Slightly
Below
the
Surface

Best Wishes

Slightly
Below
the
Surface

J.P. Riemens

Songhammer Group
2019

First Printing: 2019

ISBN 978-0-359-31228-3

Songhammer Music Group
SMG
#1 Kloepfer Rd.
Harley, Ontario N0E1E0
www.jpriemens.com

It is a lazy early Saturday. Pam is off working this morning. I'm wandering around, tidying up and listening to Patty Loveless on the stereo and finding it difficult to come up with a dedication for this book. I have been blessed with so many fine people surrounding me, it is impossible to give credit to only a few. Jon Kloepfer, for talking me into it, John Mars, Tanya Zodila, Andy Jeans, Rob DeJong, Sue Riemens for giving me their input. But fuck it. This book is dedicated to everyone I've ever met, loved and lost. If you can make it through the book, you will find the special ones.

OLD MOTHER

I have lingered here for 251 earth years. My name is Elizabeth Watts. I was born in the year seventeen sixty seven.

My spirit is intertwined with the root system of the ancient maple tree behind the old school. It reaches out into the graveyard where a stone marks my final resting place. The persistant tendrils also reach beneath the foundation of the old white building where I had spent a large portion of my life. The tree was already old when I arrived. Spared from the axe because of it's unmanageable size.

My body gave up its earthly presence on

*January the second in the year eighteen fifty six.
I was eighty nine years old. An unlikely long
life considering the hardships of the era.*

*I am not a religious person like most of the
other inhabitants of my village. It seems
ridiculous to me that the same people that
hide behind the cloak of God have forgotten
how they came to be here.*

*A good number of them are United Empire
Loyalists from the State of New York, to the
South. They were awarded their plots of land
by the Queen of England for their allegiance
leading up to the War of 1812. Many of them
were cunning opportunists, conveniently
switching sides with whomever had the upper
hand. A good number of them have murdered,
raped and hanged their neighbors in the
name of the Queen.*

*In spite of the questionable ethics of the
inhabitants, I am charged with teaching their
children to read, write and work with
numbers.*

*To the settlers in the tiny hamlet of New
Durham, known in my day as Fiddler's
Green, I am called Old Mother.*

Although time itself is of little or no

consequence to me, I am keenly aware of its passing. I have been alone for so long now, that I have taken to ponder if perhaps I may have always been just a tree and that the details of my previous existence have been nothing more than a wooden dream.

The reason for me taking the form of solid text is so as not to be left out of this story. It belongs in some small way to me as well. The author has seen fit to display me in a graceful Baskerville Boldface of which I am quite fond.

The year is nineteen sixty six and my peaceful silence is interrupted by the sound of hammer and saw. The long unoccupied school desks have been removed and sit idle in the back yard. The large slate chalk boards are tilted up against the weathered clapboard siding.

A new family has moved into the abandoned school house. In it resides a boy, who was born on the 100th anniversary of my death. An intriguing coincidence. Somehow, I feel an irrepressible desire to watch over this recently embodied soul. This is his story...

THE BOY

Mitch Ryder and The Detroit Wheels are wailing out... *devil with a blue dress, blue dress, blue dress on...* Mom is at the kitchen sink, shaking her hips...*fee fee fy fy fo fo fum...* I'm doing my best dance moves and trying to keep up...*not too skinny and not too fat, she's a real humdinger and I like it like that...* Mom does a soul spin. The dish rag rooster tails water across the kitchen...

As far back as I can remember, there was always some kind of music in our house. Mom listened to the traditional country station a lot, but most days she would tune into CKLW in Detroit. Motown – The Motor City, the home of Smokey Robinson and Marvin Gaye. When Dad came home she would flip back to the country station. One day I asked her why?

She just grinned and told me, " 'cause Dad doesn't like the colored music."

I assumed, in my five year old wisdom, that was why we also owned a black and white TV.

We lived in a rented house on a small pig farm. When I was ten, Dad bought the old school house up the road. Home.

There were no minorities where I grew up. The "Frenchies" that showed up every spring to work in tobacco didn't count 'cause that included my Mom and her relatives. School was just a bunch of white kids. The only division being farm kids or not farm kids. Life was simple.

My Father was an old man when I was born. When his first wife died of consumption, he chose to start a second family with his young bride. Mom had been Old Peter's housekeeper in 1956 where he ran his own contracting business in Langton, Ontario. They were married the same year. She was 19. He was 56. I now had four adult step-siblings older than my mother.
A lot of you may think the age difference is pretty strange, but I don't think *they* did. They were happily married for 33 years before he died.

11

According to Dad, shortly after their wedding, the Catholic priest that married them skipped town with a sack full of church money with a farmers wife on his arm. It was the talk around Langton for years. Mom said he would surely go to hell and Dad would say the man was just a 'human bean'. This confused me at the time and from then on I looked at my Mr. Potato Head and other vegetables in a different light.

People talk, I listen.

Old Peter, (the Boy calls him Dad) is kind and loving. Inside his weathered frame is the knowledge of the ancient Masons. He has been given a second chance with a new family and possesses the desire to do it right this time. The Boy does not know Peter is not his true father and the old man has never given him reason to think otherwise.

The Boy's true father was of German Ojibwe blood, given up for adoption as many children of mixed blood were. His adoptive parents were of French descent. As a young man he became a traveling musician, a handsome Gypsy with an eye for the pretty girls. He met the Boy's mother at a dance and after a whirlwind romance, left town.

Rita was from a poor family. Her father and mother had 11 children, Rita being somewhere in

12

the middle. She was raised in the woods of northern Ontario. Music and dancing was her only escape. The Boy was born when she was 18 years old, almost two years after her first child. She possesses a kind, forgiving soul and inside her tiny frame dwells the gift of patience which extends to her husband as well as the children. A most admirable quality...

Dad's everyday costume was a pair of Peabody black and white stripe bib overalls, accessorized with a red polka dot hanky in the back pocket. The hanky was used for blowing his nose, as a napkin at the dinner table or when he was working it became a knotted dew rag. 'Old Peter' was what the neighbors and everybody at the General Store called him. He was a carpenter, a mason, a soldier, a sailor, an accordion and harmonica player, a Friday night paycheck drunk and an excellent story teller. He was also a dedicated hockey enthusiast and a loyal fan of Don Messer's Jubilee (sponsored by Massey Ferguson) which came on TV before each hockey game.

I grew up believing all you needed to be a carpenter was a hammer, a hand saw and a few choice swear words on your tongue. I often practiced this technique during playtime and realized early on, the power of a well placed expletive. My older sister would always rat me out whenever she was within earshot.

There were three more siblings to come after me. Two more sisters and a brother. Older sister Diane, me, Susan, Ron and Tina in that order. My youngest sister was born in Dad's 68th year and for some reason this seemed to create a lot of excitement down at the General Store. Still having 'lead in his pencil' apparently was great cause for celebration, although I couldn't figure what that had to do with anything.

Dad worked every day until 1968 when he cut off a few fingers with one of those 'new fangled electric power saws'. It didn't stop him altogether but he more or less became a house dad after that. Mom took a job in the kitchen at the old folks home in Norwich and along with Dad's old age pension we got by just fine. As far as all us kids were concerned we had a normal childhood. I think my comfort level around old people developed early on because I was always in the presence of one. Dad was older than most of my friends grandfathers.

Mom taught me patience and compassion, Dad taught me determination, the importance of keeping your word and the value of an honest days work.

" You're only as good as your word", he would say.

After his second or third tumbler of port wine it

sounded more like "youronlysgoodsyerword", but I understood. To date, my good word is intact.

I have a vivid memory of when I was 5 years old, still living on the pig farm. I was sitting with my folks in front of the old RCA TV. A Mr. Kennedy was launching a rocket into outer space with a real monkey inside! My folks were riveted to the count down. I sat cross legged on the faded paisley linoleum floor in my cowboy pajamas, riveted to the monkey in his flashy space suit. After the launch, I asked them what would happen to the monkey and they told me I would have to wait and see. Later that day, we watched a big navy ship pull the space capsule out of the ocean, and out popped the monkey! I had no idea why anyone would want to do this.

> *...John F. Kennedy on a black and white TV,*
> *Shootin' monkey's into Heaven,*
> *Just to drop them in the sea...*

'EVERYTHING I AM'
1979 – UNRECORDED

Space ships or simply the thought of flying for that matter were inconceivable when I came to the new world in 1790. Even speaking of such wonders carried the risk of being tied to a stake and burned as a witch.

Traveling great distance took time. It took

15

thirty days and nights on a wind powered tall ship in very tight living quarters, followed by a grueling twenty day wagon journey to arrive in the new city of Montreal.

Educated in rural England, I was in my 23th year and already considered a potential spinster. I had never caught the eye of a proper suitor, nor was I desperate to. When I arrived at my new home, it was only to discover that many of the available men preferred the company of the more exotic and pliable Native Indian women over my headstrong, pious disposition. The church took the initiative to give the young native brides Christian names on their Marriage Certificates. Thus Runs-Like-A-Deer becomes Mrs Mary Smith.

It had been pre-arranged that I would be taking a position as a school marm, teaching mathematics and language skills to the rich pampered children of the local bureaucrats. My outspokenness was not an attraction to the opposite sex in a time when women were expected to be silent and endure. I did just that, but on my own terms, without the implied security of male companionship.

... but enough about me...

Nothing ever seemed to phase my Mom. You could talk to her about anything. I was taught to respect anyone who wasn't considered normal or popular and that being unique was an honorable path. She would smile and patiently explain, "Everybody is different and you should always do what you think is right for you." Every inch of her slight five foot frame defended the underdog and celebrated originality. I was always encouraged to do my own thing. I think she was a flower child before they had a name for hippies.

Her parents were a mix of French Ojibwe which was common in the North. Back then it was not in your best interest to be labeled a 'half breed' or an 'In jun', so many mixed families omitted their Native heritage. "If anybody asks you at school, tell them your dad's Italian". It is still uncomfortable for Mom to talk about, but the native connection is obvious when you look at old family photos.

Mom was an avid Elvis Presley fan. We watched every corny Elvis movie ever made, whenever they were on TV. I can recall one album in her small pile of records. "How Could 50,000,000 Fans Be Wrong?" There Elvis stands, poised in his gold lamé suit with a dozen mini Elvises floating around him in the background. We would play it on the portable Sylvania turntable. My sisters would jump around and dance and I would curl my lip, play air

17

guitar and shake a leg.

Mom has this wonderful French-Canadian accent. She taught herself English by reading comic books. Not the Superman kind, but the True Love Story ones. Growing up in English speaking Southern Ontario, us kids were not encouraged to speak French and we would always correct Mom when she got an English phrase wrong. Some of her attempts to expand her vocabulary were real doozies and we would crack up, in between giggles begging her to say it again. Mom would laugh along and shake her head, "I tell you, one of dese days you kids are going to give me a complexion!"

...Momma was a Northern girl,
Rita, Marie, Louise,
Never spent too much time in school,
That was just the Northern way,
And I was born a bunkhouse baby,
In a border town, somewhere way down South,
My Momma thought the only way to save me,
Was to put that Southern accent in my mouth...

'BUNKHOUSE BABY'
FROM THE 1991 ALBUM - MOM'S KITCHEN

THE GUITAR

Growing up out here in nowhere had it's fall-backs and it's inherent advantages. We lived just far enough from anyone that entertainment had to be self induced. You had to learn how to improvise. On Friday nights, Dad would get his accordion out and fumble through his repertoire of old war songs and polkas. Sometimes Mom would dance around with my sisters. I preferred my record player and my old portable Westinghouse radio. They were my closest friends until the day I bought a 15 dollar 'Saturn' guitar from a traveling salesman. I had earned the huge sum of currency baling hay for the neighbor next door that summer. I was eleven years old.

A guy I knew only as 'John The Salesman' was a regular visitor to our house. I don't think he had a last name. Throughout my childhood he would appear monthly with his big old car loaded to the hilt. The unorganized clutter held just about anything you could dream of. The dashboard and rear window of the old Pontiac Laurentian was a mobile showcase, filled with everything from watches and jewelry to jack knives and Zippo lighters with pin-up girls on them. He always brought in socks and balloons for us kids and my folks would feed him and put him up for the night. In spite of his soft spoken politeness, us kids always thought he was a little bit creepy. John was thin, stooped shouldered, stood over six feet tall and towered over my Mom. His clothes always looked like he had slept in them the night before, which he probably had. He sure didn't have a lot to say, especially for a salesman. He would grin at us, wink, and wiggle his little finger. Weird. The guitar he sold me was cleverly nestled under a layer of clothing and kitchen utensils in the back seat.

Once every season, when I was a child, the Gypsies would roll their colorful wagons into my little village. They would bring with them a variety of wares, cooking pots, bolts of fabric and many wonders our local blacksmith could not create. At night they would drink and dance around their little fires and the air would be filled with music and laughter. As a child I was restricted to witnessing the celebrations from a safe distance. I would fantasize of one day running away with one of the handsome dark boys and living a life of adventure. The moment never came to pass.

In the New World, I became a fully qualified spinster at the age of thirty six. There was a teaching position available in Upper Canada to the North of Lake Erie. I had developed no strong ties in Montreal and I accepted both the job and the opportunity for a change of scenery.

The Quakers had built a trade route from the small settlement of Norwich, east to the village of Burford. About half way between the two was the hamlet of Fiddlers Green (New Durham). The original log schoolhouse which doubled as the church, opened in the year of 1801 and had been destroyed by fire. The only thing that remained was a single maple tree which was spared from the axe to provide shade from the hot summer sun. It took two years of petitioning from the locals to have another school built over the ashes. In a dedication ceremony for the new White Schoolhouse S.S.#14, rows of maple saplings are planted around the perimeter of the play

21

ground.

Other than the twelve children I am assigned to, and their kin, the area is populated mostly by Native Indian tribes, driven here by the barbaric land hungry Americans and the Quakers, who seem to keep to themselves. I reside in a small single room at the back of the new building. My only window faces the old tree. This is to be my home above ground for the next 53 years.

THE LAZY SUMMER

I took great pride in earning my own money and seldom thought of asking my folks for anything they couldn't afford. The farm kids always had better stuff, but I knew how hard most of them had to work for it. All I had to do was cut grass, haul the garbage out to the burn barrel in the back yard and in the winter, carry in a container of stove oil for the kitchen heater. I never complained, in reality it was kind of nice to have something to do.

I had two buddies within a bike ride of home; Mikey and Goose. One lived at one end of my road and the other, a mile in the opposite direction. They were both dairy farm kids and always had milking or some kind of chores in their daily schedule. Not much time to listen to records or go fishing and such, but if you liked picking rocks or shoveling shit you were always welcomed to keep them company.

In the summer of 1962, when I was six, Mom would drive her old orange '53 Meteor up the road to Mike's place to buy eggs and visit with his mom, Elsie. She had 11 children. I remember a seemingly endless row of shit covered rubber boots in the mud room arranged from small to extra large. That was how I first met Mikey.

That summer, while Mom and Elsie shared tea and gossip, young Mikey and me learned how to tunnel in the hay barn and discovered that pissing on the electric cattle fence was not a such a good idea. He was around the same age as me, with a blond brush cut, a permanent grin, usually surrounded by a ring of dirt and sky blue squinty eyes.

Old John, Mikey's dad, could curse the paint off of a Farmall 140 tractor. It seemed like he practiced on Mike the most. Mike and the rest of the 'Sons O' Bitches' all worked on the farm.

In spite of Mr. K's fiery abuse of the English language, he was the best neighbor anyone could ask for. He was always there to lend a hand or lend one of his boys to anyone in need. His sons continue the tradition. I remember his laugh the most. It was a cross between a braying donkey and a punctured tire.

Mike would grow up to marry Sandy, a girlfriend of mine for the brief time I was in high school. I think they were 19 or 20 when they tied the knot. Sandy also has a special place in my life. I fell in love with every girl I ever kissed.

There is great comfort in being around the people you stumbled through adolescence with. Mike and Sandy are still a couple, more than 30 years later, surprisingly not so uncommon among many of my country friends. At times, in spite of decades of separation our connection only seemed to strengthen. This, I believe, is the measure of true friendship.

Goose, my other buddy, was a few years older than Mikey and me, which came in handy because he would be the one to get his drivers license first. He was taller than us, with broad shoulders from heavy farm work and slicked back jet black hair.

Everyone out here looked forward to their sixteenth birthday and the drivers test. I can't think of anybody who wasn't driving a month after they reached that plateau. A day after passing his drivers test we would be touring the back roads in his folks' 1962 Bel Air, headed for the WWG Drive Inn in nearby

Norwich, named after the three cute young sisters that operated it, Wendy, Wanda and Gail. I was better at chatting up the girls than my buddies, so it was always my job to 'break the ice.' This practice continued throughout our teens whenever I was around.

Long before Goose was able to drive, he had introduced me to my first 'girly' magazines which he had found under his older brothers mattress. We would spend hours thumbing through the ladies underwear section of the Eaton's catalogue after his brother got wise and found another hiding place.

Mikey occasionally supplied me with comic books and records. His live-in Grandmother would find them in his room and had declared them 'the Devils work', so instead of getting them tossed out he would just stash any questionable material over at my place. We would spend much of our time together thumbing through the latest issue of The Incredible Hulk or Daredevil, listening to records considered risqué, like Tommy James & The Shondells - Crimson & Clover. I listened to it daily and did not grow horns.

John's last name was Goossens, thus the nickname, 'Goose'. After he got his drivers license, he would take Mike and me to the Belgium Club in Delhi on Saturday nights to see some great bands. 'The Hall' had a drinking section off to the side with a small iron rail separating the drunks from the kids. I lived for those Saturday nights. I would watch and study the bands and dream of one day playing on the same stage.

The three of us country misfits became inseparable. We had our first drunk together, rode horses, smashed snowmobiles, wrecked cars and chased girls. Most of it without leaving the county. But, I'm getting ahead of myself...

When I was eleven, I landed a job with The Brantford Expositor delivering newspapers. My entire route was around three miles to deliver a measly 21 newspapers. The pay was $2.10 a week. Being a paper boy way out in the country was not very profitable. The highlight of my paper boy career happened on one 'collection day', when I would go in to get the newspaper money from my customers. Mrs. Duck had just brought home a new child. She was a supply teacher at my school, very pretty and very curvy. I dropped my bike on the front lawn and knocked on the door.

"Come right in! I'm in the kitchen!"

I stepped into the house and there she was at the kitchen table with the baby. Her shirt was unbuttoned and one of her breasts was right out there in the open! Wow! I had never seen a real boob before, let alone a teachers boob. It was marvelous! I thought my eyes from would pop right out of my head! She didn't seem to mind it at all and stuck the babies head on the tip and it began feeding. My Mom never did nothing like that! My siblings were fed from a bottle with what Mom called 'formula'. Man! This was way better!

"Come on over and see the baby", she said, as she held out the envelope with the newspaper money in it.

I couldn't believe this was happening! I nervously came in closer to see the baby, but my gaze was locked on that large teacher boob. Good God! It was bigger than the babies head! Judging by the look of contentment on the little guys face, it must have also been quite tasty. This was just like one of those dreams I'd been having late at night in the privacy of my room. The guys are never going to believe this!

Some days, I would walk the mile to Farncombe's General Store in New Durham, population 56. My folks did most of their shopping there. Food, clothing, hardware and fuel, the sign said.

Old Ross Farncombe was kind of chubby, wore his horn rimmed glasses slightly lowered on the nose of his big round head which usually displayed a kind smile. If you couldn't find what you were looking for on the shelves, Ross would open a huge trap door in the floor next to the ice cream cooler and disappear into the darkness. He would magically reappear a few minutes later with whatever object you had requested. He kept the embarrassing feminine products out of site in the mysterious back room behind the till. Over by the service garage was a single gas pump and a chalkboard that read, "Honk for Gas". Ross would only pump gas for the ladies and would tell the rest of them to "Pump yer own frikkin' gas!", then he would glance over and give me a playful wink. Even when he seemed to be grouchy, he was lightning quick with a joke.

I would get an ice cream cone and a pop for a quarter and sit on the bench inside the door and thumb through the comic books in the rack by the front window. I tended to be attracted more to Superman than Archie. The girly books were on the top shelf, far out of reach and usually covered up with a 'True Detective Magazine'. The farmers and Dad always hung out by the wood stove in the hardware section at the back of the store, telling tales, smoking cigarettes and sampling Ross's latest 'for grownups only punch'. On Sundays, the hunters would fill the back room, leaving an arsenal of rifles stacked up right beside the magazine rack at the front of the store.

The Boy seems to have developed a desire for independence at an age when he should be more interested in hunting squirrels or catching fish. For one so young he understands the concept of earning money. I watch him in his sleep and occasionally catch fleeting glimpses of his dreams. They are glorious productions, filled with treasure and far away imaginary places. I fear that one day I may lose him to his wanderlust as my consciousness is forever restricted to the confines of the ancient maple and the old school. Irregardless, the Boys dreams are a welcomed source of entertainment and my preferred escape from boredom...

Besides my paper route I tackled the drudgery by doing odd jobs for the other neighbors. Most of them ran small family farms. A few cows, some pigs and chickens, a big old tractor and about 80 acres of tillable land. Too small of a farm to sustain a living nowadays. Mikey's dad and brothers bought up most of the farms, one by one as our old neighbors retired or took jobs in the city.

I would cut grass once a week for old Mrs. Henry, with her ancient two stroke Lawn Boy push mower. I called it "Old Smokey'. The 'lawn' would better be described as a 4 acre field. My lunch break consisted of Mrs. Henry's special sandwiches, potato salad and home made lemonade. It took five hours to complete the lawn, and half of that was uphill as the yard sloped down to meet the creek. She always paid cash, four dollars and a bottle of home made dandelion wine to take home for Old Peter. Dad never failed to remind me when it was 'cutting' time.

On Christmas morning, there was always a special present for me under the tree from Mrs. Henry. One year she had collected the plastic hockey player coins that came in boxes of 'Jello' and ordered the display plaque. I had the complete collection of the Toronto Maple Leafs 1961-62 championship team. I cut her grass every summer for many years to come.

He is cutting grass now, in what used to be a beautiful stand of maple and elm trees.

Captain James Henry settled here after the war of 1812. He was awarded a 200 acre parcel of land for his service as a tall ship captain. He has built a home high on the hill facing the creek, even though he is charged with constructing a small bridge over the creek to access the road. His military training has given him cause to build on the high ground. From the vantage of his second floor window he can easily be forewarned of anyone approaching.

He grows corn and sugar cane on the cleared

31

land. The local Indians have taught him and a few other local farmers how to grow tobacco and he has found that it thrives in the rich sandy soil. He continues to require more tillable farm land and the once serene stillness is filled with the crash and groan of falling timber...

Other than Mikey and Goose, summer breaks were a write off as far as hanging out with friends. Most everyone else lived miles away.

Come September we would attend the Catholic Separate School in Burford, Blessed Sacrament. The only thing different about our school from the local public school was that we had a library and gymnasium. We did have a Nun though, Sister Noela. She was our traveling music teacher. She would show up once a week to put us through hell, singing old church songs. Sister Noela looked to be about 100 years old. A tiny, wrinkled lady in a black habit, with a voice like an overworked squeeky toy. There was zero tolerance for tomfoolery in her class. If you were out of line she would not hesitate to break a yard stick over your head. Most of the kids, including me, dreaded her classes. I'm almost positive I saw her crossing the street in Hamilton over 30 years later. She looked exactly the same.

When the school year ended, I would religiously

keep track of how many more days of summer freedom I had left on the Bank of Montreal calendar in my room. Every cent I earned in the summer of 1967, which may have added up to fifty bucks, went towards new records and 'tabulature' music books for guitar. This method displayed little pictures of where to put your fingers on the fret board and strings. Convenient, if you have not yet learned to read music. I started working on the songs that were familiar; Buffalo Springfield, The Rolling Stones, Van Morrison and The Beatles. At least that way I could play along and know if I was getting it right.

Records were about 5 dollars for an LP. I would buy them at Delhi Radio when Dad went to the liquor store for what Mom called his 'medicine'. When I wasn't inhaling tractor dust or Lawn Boy exhaust, I was in my bedroom at the top of the stairs, impatiently trying to get my fingers to trick that old piece of crap guitar into sounding like it did on the records. I wore my tattered fingertips like a badge of honor and when I got it right I would proudly audition my latest accomplishment to Mom.

Music always seemed to transport her somewhere far from the kitchen and her 5 children. I don't know exactly where that was, but when she got that distant look on her face I knew I must have been 'nailing it'. I learned to appreciate early on, the power of lyric and melody.

33

I am now quite familiar with the music of the day. In spite of my lack of a physical form, I hear everything within my range. From high in the maple, I can hear the soft music drifting over the fields from the milk house on the next farm. I am also made aware of the current political environment in this fashion. Old Peter listens to the news broadcast every morning before work and young Rita listens to music endlessly as she goes about her day.

In the evening, the family gather around a 'television'. It is similar to the radio, but with moving pictures. The children prefer to watch animated fantasy. Looney Tunes is oddly entertaining and has become a daily ritual when they return home from their schooling...

Lately the Boy's waking hours are occupied with girls and music. His dreams are saturated with more of the same. He spends hours in his room playing his guitar. Sometimes repeating the same song over and over until I wish I was somewhere else.

As a young lady, I was expected to play the piano as was every cultured lady. My playing was more mechanical than musical and though I tolerated the weekly lessons, I soon lost interest. Slowly the Boy's new obsession becomes infectious and I begin to share in his excitement. I am mystified as the songs take shape and I experience something akin to physical joy...

34

GROWN UP JOB

In my 13th year, I got my first job in tobacco. I was the 'boat unloader'. The 'boat' is a long, narrow container on wooden runners that the huge workhorse pulled through the rows for the 'primers' to fill. The girls on the 'table gang' handed leaves, three at time to the 'tyer' who tied the tobacco on sticks with blinding speed. The sticks would then be sent up a conveyor belt to be hung in the kiln by the 'kiln hanger'. My job was to unload the tobacco onto the table for the girls, seven days a week until it was over, around 5 or 6 weeks later.

The primers that year had come up from Georgia, down south, along with the old Southern Cureman. It seemed back then, all curemen were required to have a southern accent. The primers would throw little gifts from the field into the 'boat' for me and the gang. A garter snake or two, but mostly giant, green tobacco worms that were just as green on the inside when you splattered them on the wall of the kiln. In return, we would send them a jug of cold water and snacks.

The old cureman, Mr. Walker, slept in a tiny shack in the kiln yard and hung around with us a lot during the day. He had this great southern drawl, "Mahin oh mahin, the frowgs were just a hollerin' last naght, I coutn't slip a wank." He enjoyed sipping bourbon and whittling 'nothin' 'n particular' between his rounds. If things weren't going his way, he would look down at his feet, shake his head and exclaim, "Now, don't that make the cheese more bindin'?"

Two of the leaf handers on the table were the Hephner twins. Sixteen year old bookend vixens. God, they were hot! They shared identical smiles and many times wore similar clothes. Perfection in stereo. I was twice smitten. This made getting up for work every morning a breeze. I often got there ahead of the rest of the crew every morning so that I could get a chance talk to the girls before the first load of tobacco came in. My new found adolescent yearnings were almost impossible to contain and I would fantasize endlessly about them. It was a long *hard* summer, if you get my drift.

In our township and down to the north shore of Lake Erie, us tobacco kids got to start the school year two weeks later than the rest. This was a bonus for me. I was learning a lot more about life from the older kids in the tobacco gang, and an extra two weeks under the spell of the Hephner twins was preferable over just about anything.

I earned a whopping six hundred dollars that summer. My older sister and I bought Mom a new 26 inch console television that fall. It was still black and white.

I would revisit the tobacco fields many times growing up. Besides the harvest there were many other jobs that could keep you busy for almost 9 months of the year. Some lasted only a week or two. You could steam greenhouses, work in planting, irrigate, hoe, top, sucker. After harvest you could work in the 'strip room', grading and baling the cured tobacco. A great way to make enough money to leave town. It was a way of life for many folks in my part of the country. People came from everywhere to work in the fields. I'm sure, if you ask around in Southern Ontario there is always someone in the room who has a tobacco story.

J.P. Riemens

...Lazy summer afternoon,
School is out and harvest starts real soon,
There's a farm by the lake, with a job for me,
There's a dance hall on the beach,
They've always got a real good band,
That's where I first saw her swayin' in the sand..

DOVER GIRL
2006-FROM THE ALBUM-PLAIN AND SIMPLE.

VISON QUEST

I strongly believe, my early experiences with LSD are pivotal to who I am today. What I'm not sure of is whether it has contributed to my successes or to my failures. With certainty, my desired path had become clear and in focus. As shocking as this may seem to some of you, this was the end of 60's, a time before social media and the internet. The news was dominated by reports from Viet Nam, where kids not much older than me were dying every day. The students were demonstrating for an end to the war, racial equality, women lib and social change. The music on the radio was shifting from Elvis and the Beatles to Led Zepplin, Janis Joplin and Frank Zappa. On TV, it was Rowan and Martin's Laugh-In, Buffalo Springfield was on the Red Skelton Show and The Band was on Ed

Sullivan.

Out here in Harley, we lived in a very small world surrounded by cattle and tobacco farms, far from any urban sprawl. Books, television and radio were the only outside influence. Burford, population 1200, was the nearest town. The new Catholic School was there as well as the High School. Sprowls Department Store stood on the main intersection at the only traffic light. There was a bakery, a post office, a bowling alley and Hunt's Restaurant where us kids would sometimes sit at the long lunch counter with a large plate of 25 cent french fries and gravy. All that stuff happening south of the border seemed to be a world away.

I was introduced to LSD by my school chum's older brother, Frank. It was the fall of '69, I was 13. It was pure white clinical, not the kind that had happy faces or strawberries stamped on them. I took it over at the Burford Fair Grounds where us kids would gather under the shelter of the grandstand to smoke cigarettes and pass around bottles of cheap wine, pretending to be grown ups. I walked the seven long miles home that afternoon. What a glorious autumn day! For the first time I was totally aware of the multicolored landscape and how it all fit together. It felt like I was in a gigantic picture puzzle and we were all somehow connected. Passing by an undulating green pasture, there was a group of jet black horses framed by a paisley blue sky. A young colt bucked and kicked at the sky. I shared the same exhilaration. It wasn't so boring out here after all!

When I finally got home I managed to keep it together until it was time for the weekly Sunday ritual. The family would retire to the living room after dinner to watch Disney's 'Wonderful World of Colour', which wasn't in colour at all on our TV. I excused myself from my older sister's accusing scrutiny and retired to the sanctity my room.

They say we only use ten percent of our brain and I often wondered what the rest of that gray matter was for. Until that day. My brain was firing on all cylinders. I envisioned an endless hallway with a million doors. LSD provided the master key, to open any one...

What powerful magic is this? I find myself in a beautiful furnished room somewhere inside of the Boy's mind. I am a young girl of perhaps 12 or 13. I have grown unfamiliar to the feel of gravity, though I am surprisingly light on my feet, twirling in circles, arms outstretched. My flowered gown, although very pleasing is cut scandalously short just below the knees. I am not overly concerned. This is a safe place.
I peek out the window and see the Boy's room on the other side. I notice an ornate door

41

opposite the window. I am almost certain, if I were to open it and look out into the hall, I would come face to face with the Boy.

Perhaps he would join me in the dance. The temptation is hard to ignore, but somehow I sense the time is not right and I manage to resist...

I opened one door to find a parallel world where everything and everyone was animated, like a R. Crumb comic. I liked it in there. It was a happy place. I could defy gravity and fly without effort into the endless cartoon sky. Behind other doors were abstract images, my school teachers in a classroom where the words come out of their mouths into cartoon balloons and melt like ice cream into sticky puddles around their feet. Another room displayed an elaborate blue print of how everything fit together, an endless illustration of gears and circuitry illuminated in detailed neon ecstasy. Down the hall I had a curious urge to open yet another door, where I sensed someone very special was waiting for me, but I was unsure about meeting anyone in my present condition. I hesitated and continued in the opposite direction.

This was a vision quest, an ancient calling. The flood gates had burst. I was no longer alone in the vast universe and fearless of what it may deal out. It occurred to me that, if only for a moment or two, I had been to a place that every major prophet from Jesus Christ to Budda had left their footprint. This day changes everything. From this moment on, I would see things in a different light.

NEW KID IN TOWN

I had saved enough money that summer to buy a decent guitar for $99.99, from the Simpson Sears mail order catalog. We picked it up at the train station in nearby Norwich. It was 1969. I bought some cool clothes from Gamble's Department Store in Brantford, striped bell bottoms with matching vests like 'The Monkees', a wide studded belt and Beatle boots with zippers on the side. It created quite a distraction for some of the teachers at Blessed Sacrament School in Burford. We weren't the 'uniformed Catholics' you would associate with most Separate Schools. There was no outlined dress code, as long as things remained relatively 'normal', but on the first day of grade 7, the teacher made me sit in the hall because I was wearing bell bottoms. Satan's pants I was told. A dreaded visit to the Principal Hubbert's office proved beneficial however. When it was revealed I had earned the money to buy my own school clothes, I was awarded a level of respect from the staff and they had no choice but to allow my devilish garb. Meanwhile, I was officially deemed a rebel by my classmates. I had beat the system just like those student protesters on the news. When I returned the next day the girls in class suddenly took greater interest.

There was one girl I had a crush on. Her name was Joanne. Her folks were tobacco farmers and I was just a poor carpenters kid. Not a good match. The 'rich' kids all stuck together, not that they were nasty or anything, they just didn't go out of their way to hang out with the rest of us. I didn't fit in with their crowd, but Joanne told me one day that she thought I wore the coolest clothes, and that was good enough for me. Unfortunately, a growth spurt half way through the school year rendered the pants about 2 inches too short and the shoes way too tight. My hair was in the middle of that awkward stage between short and long. I must have looked ridiculous. I wore the clothes and the uncomfortable footwear anyway. Mom, God bless her, sewed paisley extensions onto the bottoms of my pants. In my mind, I felt like the coolest kid in class.

THE MISSION

One night, I was under the blankets with my old Westinghouse radio, trying to tune into anything new from across the lake in Buffalo, when I caught a show entirely devoted to James Taylor's new record. "Mud Slide Slim". It was 1970. I had just completed grade 8.

Wow! I had never heard of this guy before. His storytelling and imagery were mesmerizing. The sparse musical accompaniment and acoustic guitar sent chills down my spine. I was certain that I could play that stuff. It set the bar for what was to become a lifelong obsession. In that moment, I knew exactly what I was going to do. I was going to be the long haired, guitar playing, songwriter that girls swooned over and guys envied. Maybe even get rich and famous!

A few years later I would discover Tom Waites, then Gram Parsons, Neil Young and John Prine. All of them would have an impact on my songwriting, but the seeds were planted back then in my room, listening to Sweet Baby James.

When I was this age, my dreams were of a handsome prince or a noble knight on a white stallion. I never had visions of being a teacher. Music was almost nonexistent in my village, except for the church choir and a particularly handsome tinker who would visit on his monthly route. He played an ornate Lute and told tales of love, war and magic. I was quite enchanted and foolishly fantasized of one day running away with him. (a recurring theme, that in addition to the tinker, included almost any kind stranger that could offer an escape from this tiny village.)

Mother explained to me that most musicians were opportunistic Gypsy's and therefore not deemed honorable or trustworthy. Regardless, I secretly looked forward with great anticipation for the next performance...

TRANSFORMATION

No life changing plans turn out to be easy. Dreams can be slippery little devils. You would think the long hair would have been a breeze, I was half way there, but in a community where everybody looked and dressed the same, it was still frowned upon. Anything that upset the norm was discouraged. Change was not something to desire. Try not to stick out. Follow in your fathers footsteps and don't rock the boat. I was determined not to be a willing victim of that small town inertia, at whatever cost.

Mom was sympathetic to my new aspirations and let me skip her regular hair cutting sessions and with some help from my uncle's Brylcream (A Little Dab'l Do Ya), I kept my hair slicked back behind my ears so Dad wouldn't be the wiser. I found out much later that I wasn't fooling anyone. Dad used to get a kick out of my clever disguise. He had played in many dance hall bands throughout the 30's, 40's and 50's and I think he was a lot more open minded than he let on. I found some pictures of him in the 20's. His straight unkempt strawberry blond hair hung down low across his forehead and was cut short on the sides like the old banks robbers and jazz musicians of the era. He was cool.

Swimming against the tide proved to be a daunting task. Even some of my closest friends didn't get it. The few that did could not offer any support without condemning themselves to the same harassment. In this rural Eden, I was always one step away from being thrown out of the Garden.

J.P. Riemens

...Growing up in nowhere,
Ain't as easy as it seems,
The kids in town don't understand,
My little country dreams,
I want to see it all,
I don't want to watch the world go by,
And Lonely Joan says, when your gone,
I promise I won't cry...

LONELY JOAN
2013 FROM THE ALBUM -NO FILTER

HOLDING ON BY A THREAD

My last summer as a boy was, and still remains slightly out of focus. I went through all of the motions expected for a boy of fifteen and continued to practice my guitar as usual, but it felt as if I was in a cloud. I remember discovering the freedom of hitch hiking and going on little trips to local music festivals around Southern Ontario, remembering little of the performances, but the joy of being a part of the occasion. I spent an abnormal amount of time alone in my room wondering how I could have turned into such a klutz. Damn this growth spurt. I couldn't even walk right. It seemed like I had somebody else's legs and my head looked too big for my body. I really didn't want to be seen by any of my friends. Thank God school was finally out.

In a blink, Harvest was approaching. I was offered a job on my godfather's farm in Fairground, Ontario, near Sand Hills Park on Lake Erie. This proved to be an easy way to get away from everybody that knew me until my body grew into itself and felt normal again.

Paul Vincent, my Godfather, was a hardworking, determined French Canadian, proficient in swearing in both official languages. He was also a great guitar player and was part of a local band, The Continentals. They played all of the local dance halls. My job was to be his helper through the season, keeping the machinery greased and oiled and helping to fix anything that needed fixing. He didn't particularly approve of my long hair, but never tortured me about it other than nicknaming me, Beatnik.

It wasn't an easy ride. He expected the same from me as the rest of the men on the farm and I was treated as such. I slept in the bunkhouse with all the other workers. They were all from Quebec and none of them spoke English. They called me Beatnik, too, with emphasis on the second syllable.

My Godfather taught me the art of kiln hanging and

the secrets of curing tobacco that summer. One of our responsibilities was to empty the kiln after the tobacco was cured. With him on the wagon, he showed me how to handle two sticks at a time and pass them down for him to pile. As I got deeper into the kiln he handed me boards to walk on and an aluminum slide positioned to deliver the sticks. The first kiln took most of a morning to completely empty. He patiently explained how a broken stick or sloppy hanging could damage the delicate curing process. I basically learned how to hang a kiln in reverse. By the end of the season the two of us could empty a complete kiln in under an hour.

Near the end of the season on those cold September mornings, the kiln would have to be steamed before removing the brittle golden tobacco. The steamer looked like a miniature locomotive. A large hose fed the steam into the kiln and after a while the tobacco was softened enough to handle. We would start at 5am so the kiln would be ready for the workers at 7. I would step out of the cold morning air into a cloud of steam and hand out the sticks. Steam and sweat, the sun slowly peeking into the open doorway. The sweet smell of the cured tobacco in the early autumn air. When we were finished we would join the workers in the farmhouse for a huge country breakfast. A fond memory.

One day, near the end of the season, I realized I was being treated the same as the rest of the men, an equal, doing a man's work. My confusion dissipated. I was no longer clumsy or awkward. It seems, almost overnight my chest had widened to fit my arms and head. My legs seemed to be the right size and moved with an effortless grace. I was no longer a boy.

The Boy is back home. Preparing for the big day. Tomorrow he begins High School. He is not afraid. Asleep, he dreams.

He is horizontal and floating in the air, weightless, facing skyward. A thin silken rope envelopes his body, wrapped around him from head to toe like a cocoon. He twists himself to turn and face the ground only to see his younger twin desperately holding on to the exposed end of the rope five feet below. As their eyes lock he sees only the billowy clouds below them.

As if on an invisible rotisserie the weight of the younger boy below begins to slowly unravel the rope and he begins to spin, gradually increasing speed. With each revolution he sees the young boy falling further and further away from him until finally the rope becomes detached and leaves his body. He makes an effort to grasp the loose end, but fails. He does not fall, but floats down through the clouds and

54

lands softly on the ground beside the loose pile of discarded rope.

The boy is nowhere to be found. The young man rises to his feet...

BDHS

By the time I got to Burford District High School in 1971, I had it down. The hair was no longer an issue, except for having the odd redneck calling me a freak. It had grown long and curly to my shoulders. I had a pair of patched blue jeans like Neil Young, suspenders like James Taylor and I was on my way to cool-dom, no matter what.

I was walking to the General Store in New Durham that summer and noticed one of the neighbors watching me pass by from behind a closed window, as if they feared I was some kind of demonic threat. The summer before, I was in their kitchen being offered cookies. Most of the other locals eyed me with curious caution as did my school teachers and a lot of the other kids.

Some of the girls would whisper to each other and giggle when they passed me in the hall.

High school was nothing more than a distraction. I got good grades without studying. I understood the answers the teachers wanted to hear and played along with their vaporous little games. It was so painfully boring that I would often take small doses of LSD just to make it through the day. This made science class almost enjoyable.

I got ribbed a lot because I took music class instead of shop. "It just isn't manly", the other guys would say. I told my tormentors that I was really just there for the chicks. Hell, Johnny Givens and me were the only boys in a classroom of 35. How's that for manly?

Johnny was that kid on Don Messers Jubilee that came on to play a fiddle tune every week. He had already won many fiddle competitions and even met Johnny Cash. Johnny Givens didn't give a fuck what anybody said. Dad said he was famous and made me come and watch whenever he was on the TV show.

Our music teacher's name was Mr. Joe Blow. (really) Now, this guy was strange, and to me, resembled the old blood hound on the Beverly Hillbillies TV show. He would address the class, jowls a-flappin' "Ahhh-hellow, Ahhh, my name is Mr. Ahhh, Bahhhlow". In spite of his awkward social skills he was a great music teacher. Clearly it was his passion. He taught us all how to read music and sing.

We lived too far away from town for me to regularly participate in any after school activities. Instead of playing on the football or soccer team, I would usually take the school bus home, 7 miles out, go to my room and listen to records. I had three records that I almost wore out, Neil Youngs' first solo album, James Taylor's, 'Mudslide Slim' and The Band, 'Music From Big Pink'. The rest of the time I would practice on my new Sears guitar and dream of stardom.

...He sings in the kitchen,
To his family and friends,
And anyone else who might stop and drop in,
And the closest he gets to those neon lights
Is a full moon in August,
On a hot summers night...

FULL MOON IN AUGUST
1996 – FROM THE ALBUM -FULL MOON IN AUGUST

.

With thick layered skin and a quick sense of humor, I figured I was the hippest freshman ever. A lot of girls liked me, close friends surrounded me, teachers tolerated me because I got good grades. I had managed to outwit or befriend the bullies and not get my ass kicked, and in my village, drinking and fighting was considered a time honored tradition and a reliable cure for boredom. Quite an accomplishment. Daydreaming became my new major. I would sit at the back of the class and imagine I was on a stage with a loud band behind me and throngs of admirers in the front row. Sometimes I would just skip out for the day with a girlfriend and go down to Whitemans Creek to make out. The study of the female anatomy was not part of the required curriculum but something I took great interest in. We always made sure we were back in time to catch the bus home.

...Lonely Joan was a country girl,
She grew up down the road,
When we were young, we had some fun,
Just me and Lonely Joan,
Skippin' school and skippin' stones,
Down by the river bank,
Makin' love to Lonely Joan, put a fire in my tank...

LONELY JOAN
2013 -FROM THE ALBUM -NO FILTER

On my 16th birthday, I quit school and got my drivers license. I had not completed grade ten.

SCHOOL'S OUT FOREVER

My old friend Mikey from up the road had quit school just before me and got a job at a local machine shop in Burford. This didn't fare well with his folks who wouldn't have minded him quitting if his intent was to help out on the farm, but he had other plans. He said he would get me in.

Being a school teacher for most of my life. I am apprehensive about this sudden move. The Boy is a good student. It is not my intent to disagree with his decision even if it could be acknowledged, after all, most of my students were only taught to read, write and work with numbers. It was not my obligation to teach them anything more. To spark their curiosity or wanderlust may have lured them away from where they were most needed. Most of the boys were expected to go back to the farm. The average male student left school at 14 or 15, as soon as he was able to keep up with the adults. Many of the girls married and were with child before they could complete their studies.

In the Boy's case I trust that a good student is still a good student, and living in the real world will offer a learning experience that cannot be taught in the traditional classroom...

The new boss, Mr. Fowler was a great teacher and I was soon running a metal lathe and all kinds of other machine shop wonders. This was way better than anything I heard about happening in shop class. I fell in love with the gears and sprockets that brought life to the shop in showers of spark and smoke. I was a natural. He offered to sponsor me for an apprenticeship, which was tempting, but I wasn't ready to give up my music dream just yet. I hadn't even really got started. I chose to give it a year.

It was a short year. Unfortunately, in Burford there were not many other musicians to share my aspirations with. In fact, there was no one to be found. If I was going to do this music thing, I had to 'Get out of Dodge.' My plan of attack was to pack my bag, hit the road and see the country. I would become a singing troubadour just like Bob Dylan or Woody Guthrie before him. I needed to experience things that I could write about. I had proven I could hold down an adult job, but that was no excuse to give up my dream. So one warm late spring day, with my backpack and guitar, I headed west on the Harley Road and into the unknown.

...Go West, go West, The call of the wild,
The land of the setting sun,
With open arms, we'll take you child,
And show you how it's done...

BONNIE
2000 -FROM THE ALBUM - GIRLS

If my folks were worried, they didn't show it. After all, they had come from big families and had also left home in their teens. Mom had migrated south to work in tobacco and pick fruit. Dad had left Holland at 16 and sailed with the merchant marines before settling in Canada. My older sister had moved out at 17 and was doing well on her own. To them as with many parents of that era, leaving the nest was a necessary part of growing up.

My 'big city' experience, to date was limited, consisting of a few trips to Toronto and Ottawa on chaperoned bus trips from school and with Goose in his fathers '62 Chev cruising around Brantford on Friday nights. I wasn't exactly a 'Man of the World' yet, but I was ready for anything. 'I have nothing to fear', was my mantra.

I blindly stuck out my thumb, with nothing more
than a change of clothes, my guitar,
65 dollars and a picture of home.

I have feared that this day would come. The Boy has become his own person, with a headstrong goal and a fearless heart. His dreams shall belong to him alone while he is away. The roots of the old maple reach out and gain new ground, but the extent of my travel is measured in inches. If somehow I could leave this place and to join him on the journey I would go without hesitation.

I shall have to be content watching over his family, although I am not attached to them with the same intimacy. I hear and observe. The younger ones playful laughter provides a nostalgic ambiance to the old school...

THE ROAD

Pierre Elliot Trudeau was Prime Minister and was pouring our tax dollars into all kinds of youth social programs. There was a youth hostel in practically every town in the country. They were often operated in the summer by kids not much older than me. It was too cool!

Hitch hiking was now widely accepted. The associated horror stories were usually circulated by over protective parents or school teachers who had never been away from the relative safety of the school system. Across the country, it was an age of freedom and discovery for thousands of wide eyed kids just like me.

You never get lonely on the road. Every ride holds

the promise of a new story. Strangers trapped in the confines of an automobile tend to engage in conversations that they would normally only share with trusted confidants. Practicing my social skills, I would try to find something in common to break the ice and put my ride at ease. If you give the required responses and ask the right questions, the rewards can be a story worthy of any Steven King novel.

The hostels cost between 50 cents to a dollar for a safe place to sleep and a meal, but most times it didn't cost a penny if you had a guitar and played a few songs for the staff and guests. You could meet every kind of person there, foreign college students, migrant workers, runaways, other musicians and of course lots of girls. I found out early on that it was easier to get a ride if you had a girl with you. I had more than my share of female companionship, some for a day or two and some only to the next town. This spawned a lot of short term roadside romance and great fodder for unrequited love songs.

> ...And like an angel from heaven,
> She lets go my hand,
> She says, she'll be here, waiting next year,
> But both of us know, this is goodbye,
> And the love that we made was real...

SOUTHERN ONTARIO SUNSET
2006-FROM THE ALBUM-PLAIN AND SIMPLE

Out here, you can be whoever you want, without compromise. There was no one to remind you of who you may have been back in the awkward days. It was liberating. I was a songwriter, a troubadour, a child of the universe, although at the time, I had only just begun the journey and had written only a handful of songs. I often thought of my friends back home living their pre-determined lives, wondering if they were dreaming of what my life must be like.

Too many times I remember some old farmer saying, "I wish I had of done that when I was your age." So I made a promise to myself. That phrase would never cross my lips.

I would rather try and fail than live with regret.

NORTHERN ONTARIO

Northern Ontario is gigantic. Mile after endless mile, occasionally broken up by a small town or cluster of modest homes. The two lane road and parallel train track slashes its corridor through three hundred and twelve thousand square miles of tree after tree, rock after rock, lake after lake. Green, gray, blue, green, gray, blue, the sweet smell of pine, granite and water.

Three days into my journey and I wasn't even half way through it when I got dropped off in Wawa, Ontario. There is a statue of a giant Canada Goose taking flight at the turn-off. Wawa was a notorious place for not being able to get a ride. Kelly Jay from the band Crowbar even had a song about it, "I'll catch up to you, Tit's up on the pavement, in

Wawa, Ontari-ari-o!" So at the very beginning of my adventure, here I was in this northern vortex. It was said it sucks up hitchhikers only to spit them out weeks later or as legend has it sometimes never. I decided to just keep walking away from the goose until somebody picked me up. Between the passing cars I pulled out my guitar and trudged along in the late afternoon stillness, practicing my finger picking patterns. The mindless repetition seemed an appropriate and productive way to fight the boredom. The rest of the day passed by and so did the cars. I had long left behind any signs of civilization. Darkness was approaching and there I was, in a vast alien world of tree and stone, my only company, an occasional bothersome bug. The stars above were my the only source of light. I was getting pretty spooked. When the silence is disrupted by a crash and a grunt in the bush, I imagine a huge black bear or a moose stumbling through the forest towards me. The song "Tit's Up On The Pavement" was on an endless loop, playing over and over in my head. I strategically lit a cigarette whenever a car approached so the driver would see me. The fire flies would signal back with every puff and the cars flew by like I was just another big ass-lit insect. Around midnight, I finally got a ride. What a relief. All I could think of was the tragic newspaper headline: "Burford Area Youth Found – chewed carcass, 3 songs and a guitar are discovered in a ditch somewhere in BumFuck Ontario". Not the future I had in mind.

In the present, I am with the Boy as he remembers this ordeal. I relive my introduction to the New World. The desolation the Boy describes is a mirror image of what I encounter between Halifax and my new home in Montreal in the year 1790. The vast wilderness is relentless in its continuity.

It is difficult to measure our progress as we travel, as if we are in a stage play with a painted backdrop that never changes. Rock, tree and water. The only sign of civilization, the narrow path, an occasional fur trappers hovel or small Indian encampment...

My ride was with well worn old carny who called himself Memphis. He recited a treasure chest of bawdy stories about carny life while he sipped straight Triple-X whiskey from the bottle. His abused '63 Lincoln Continental was littered with old carnival posters and a variety of styrofoam fast food containers. The car quietly floated through the night like a huge mechanical ghost. The stories he told were far better than any paperback adventure I had ever read. It's always enjoyable hearing a story told from the perspective of the lead character. His ragged appearance and endless narration carved its way through the darkness surrounding us, and in some way reminded me of the great OZ. With one gold tooth occasionally reflected in the dashboard lights, he spouted tales of romantically starved bearded ladies, broken hearts and knife fights with small town thugs. He drove an increasingly crooked path through the night, educating me on the advantages of perpetual motion and how to survive as a stranger in a strange land, how to separate a 'mark' from his money and how to say goodbye to a one night stand. His delivery, punctuated with a chubby six gun pointed finger, intensifying with every sip.

Around 10am the next morning we swerved into the relative safety of Dryden, Ontario. The end of the line for my now drunken orator. Memphis was headed to the local fair ground to make ready the lot for the carnival trucks arriving later that day and I assumed, a well deserved nap. My head was hurting from the endless influx of pertinent information and in addition to the dull throb, the town smelled like you had eaten a box of wooden matches and farted. "Eau Du Pulp Mill".

Many miles back in a coffee shop, I had overheard a guy telling a joke. "This couple are making out in a car and the girl says, "Kiss me where is smells", so he drove her to Dryden." Hyuk hyuk!

THE BIG FISH

I walked about a half mile to a sleepy little gas station/diner on the outskirts of 'Stinkytown'. The sign outside read, 'Eat Here and Get Gas'. Over a cup of bad coffee and a greasy grilled cheese sandwich I struck up a conversation with a young Native guy at the counter. Actually, he initiated it by sliding the ketchup over and telling me to shake it up good. "I don't know what that clear shit is that comes out first if you don't, but it's nasty."

He was headed to the Rez just outside of Kenora and kindly offered me a short ride. His old pickup truck had no radio and he had hung a string of small bells from the rearview mirror to disrupt the silence. He was nice guy, only a few years older than me. Soft spoken and to the point, his calm voice was a welcomed contrast to the conversational acrobatics of my previous traveling companion. He confessed he too had dreamed of travel but was content with his surroundings and could see no immediate reason to unearth his roots. When he dropped me off he gave me five bucks for lunch and wished me good luck on my journey.

It was a beautiful day and the walk into the little town in The Lake Of The Woods was picture perfect. The sky was a deep cloudless blue and the distance between here and Dreyden had reintroduced the sweet scent of pine and wet earth. The twenty minute hike was just what I needed to recharge. The sudden lack of conversation was welcomed.

Before 1905, Kenora was known as Rat Portage and belonged to the province of Manitoba. I read this historical fact on one of the small roadside plaques that dot the Trans Canada Highway.

At the 'Welcome to Kenora' sign, I heard a big boom and thought nothing of it. "Likely a road crew blasting rock", I muttered to myself, but when I entered Main Street I knew something wasn't right. I thought perhaps my lack of sleep had caught up with me and I was in some kind of slow motion waking dream. There were 20 dollars bills lazily floating through the air! I managed to catch a few in disbelief. A lot of stores along the block had broken windows. Sirens were sirening, cop cars with flashing lights, and fire trucks were roaring in to block off both sides of the street. I thought for a brief moment that I had been magically transported into the middle of a Clint Eastwood 'Dirty Harry' cop movie.

As it turns out, a bad guy had robbed the local bank with a bomb strapped to his body and according to the locals, it accidentally went off when he got safely into the center of the street. Kinda like a Wile E.Coyote screw up in a Road Runner cartoon. Nasty! How the locals came to the conclusion that it was accidental, I'll never know, but it led me to believe that they were somehow involved.

First chance I got, I examined the twenties to make sure nothing foreign was stuck to them and stashed them in my backpack. I skirted around the block and said my good bye to the Big Fish and got a another ride at the western edge of town.

Like Wawa's giant goose, a lot of Northern towns have big statues, I guess for tourists to take pictures of. Blind River has a Giant Thermometer, Mattawa has Big Joe Mufferaw, Sudbury has the Big Nickel, and Kenora has a Giant Fish. Because of it's former name, I've always thought that a Giant Rat would be have been more appropriate.

73

My days are now spent in the company of the Boy's brother and sisters. The younger brother has recently discovered masturbation and I leave him to his selfish indulgence. The two youger girls are in the kitchen with Rita attempting to bake cookies, but much of the dough does not get to oven. Rita patiently mixes up another batch.

Old Peter is at his regular spot, leaning on the kitchen island, sipping cold, black coffee and reading a Louis L'Amour paperback. The children are slowly becoming young adults. As the days become weeks I wait in anticipation for news of the Boy's travels and his safe return...

THE PRAIRIES

My new mode of travel was in a banana yellow
VW bug convertible with a guy not much older
than me from Boston, Massachusetts. He had long
wavy black hair tucked into a Red Sox cap and a
funny accent that I had only ever heard on
television.

He said stuff like; "Pawly, get in the Kaa! Wouldja
like a drink of watta?".

We listened to Chicago Transit Authority on the 8
track all the way to Winnipeg while he narrated
the history of everyone in the group. I had never
met a more informed Chicago fanatic from Boston
before or since. (I might add, the group 'Boston'
had yet to be enter the picture.) This guy was

surely CTA's biggest fan. He was following the band's cross country North American tour and decided to detour through Canada for a stretch.

An hour out of Kenora is another giant sign, 'Welcome To Manitoba'. I was about to step out of Ontario for the first time.

The occasional travelers may stop here to have their picture taken by the sign but there is more to the spot than meets the eye. In a small unmarked clearing behind the sign you will find messages and greetings from fellow travelers. The tradition continues to this day.

Not twenty minutes past the border, the tree line ends abruptly. Forest. No forest. It is replaced by a flat, desolate landscape that stretches forever westward.

"I wonder who cuts the grass?", I joked.

My Bostonian friend laughed and introduced the next Chicago song, the 8 track clicks... On to Winnipeg with "25 or 6 to 4" blaring through the speakers.

The city was massive! It loomed out of the prairie horizon like Godzilla rising from the ocean floor. There where paddle wheel river boats, more than one French section, Portage and Main, the center of town, and places on the banks of the Assiniboine in the north east end, you should know to avoid...

> *...I've been to the bottom of the earth,*
> *Winnipeg Manitoba, To the Northeast end,*
> *Where every demon has a home,*
> *Police tape and razor wire,*
> *Gangs that set your house on fire,*
> *And streets you don't want to walk alone...*

WAITING FOR THE BOOM
2010- FROM THE ALBUM -DIRTY SUNSET

You never hear much about Winnipeg back home. It's always 'Toronto this' or 'Toronto that', still is, but Winnipeg, my God! All the fine music that was pouring out of that town in the 70's could have washed Toronto up the St. Lawrence into New Brunswick. I decided to hang out for a while and explore and said goodbye to my Bostonian Chicago fan. Strains of 'Does Anybody Really Know What Time It is' faded into the distance along with the familiar chirp of the VW.

I recall someone telling me that there was around 600 live music venues in this town. Filled with inspiration I jumped right in and started number 601 right there on the street corner. People passing by on the busy sidewalk would stop for a few moments, listen, and then to my surprise throw loose change into my open guitar case. This was my first ever street singing gig. What a concept! What a town! I found a whole culture of street performers all over the downtown area and quickly joined their ranks.

We would meet daily in the park during the down time between 2 and 3pm to trade songs and stories. There were a few funky coffee houses off on the back streets, 'The Ting' and 'The Banyan Tree'. They generously offered you a free meal for a few songs. They were both tiny places and had a policy of charging 15 cents an hour to their patrons to discourage any 'table hogs'. Of course they couldn't feed all of us, so every afternoon we picked straws to see who would have the honour.

The best time to play was between 11 until 2pm to catch the lunch crowd. 3 to 6pm caught everyone leaving work from the offices. After a while you discover the best spots to make money, but you have to wait your turn to get the desirable location. It's a seniority thing. I would sometimes go further down the block to play while I waited my turn. That's how I met Holley.

She wasn't a singer,

"Hey kid, this is my corner, shove off!"

The girl looked annoyed. All I saw was a well dressed, dark haired beauty without an instrument.

I replied in honest confusion, "Oh! I'm really sorry, miss, what do you play?"

"Whatever they want me to, silly", she gave me a naughty grin.

Green as I was, it took a while for me to figure out what she meant. Suddenly it hit me. Whoa! They didn't have hookers where I came from. Rumours of loose women floated around Burford but usually they didn't require payment. This was Big City stuff.

Holley looked perplexed and laughed,"Listen kid, you have to be street smart to survive in this town and as far as I can tell, you're nothing but street stupid."

I didn't have an answer for her. I just stood there with my mouth open like a hungry guppy.

She looked amused and shook her head, "What the hell, business is slow today, you'd better come along with me."

She kindly offered to show me my way around, "so

you don't get yourself killed" and then brought me home to meet her room mate like I was a stray dog.

"Look what I found out on the street! Isn't he cute! I think he's hungry, lets give him a bath!"

I was unofficially adopted.

Lucy, her girlfriend was a tiny soft spoken rural Manitoba girl, and quick to laugh. She studied and kept house and I sang on the street during the day. I always made enough money to buy groceries, which I would bring home to cook for them. I like to pull my weight, besides, being in the kitchen always reminded me of Mom. I never admitted it before, but I kind of missed her.

Holley was putting her friend Lucy through business school. The two girls had big dreams of opening their own art shop when she graduated and they had saved enough up enough money. Holley worked mostly days. Her clients, business men on their lunch or extended coffee breaks. She said it was too dangerous to work evenings.

"And listen", she would tell me, "Don't hang out near Portage and Main after dark and stay away from Memorial Park at night. It's crawling with rubbies and gay guys cruising around looking for nice innocent boys like you."

At night I stayed indoors. I would usually try out my new songs on the ladies after the dinner dishes and Holley would end the evening telling hilarious stories about her exploits with some of her 'Johns'.

In spite of it's bad night time reputation, Memorial Park in the daylight was my favourite place to busk. Across the street was head quarters for The Great West Life Insurance Company and Labatt brewery. All the young secretaries would come to the park for lunch and I would play for them. Because of the university here, most of them had come here from small rural towns across the prairies and were as in awe of the big city as I was. They were very generous, and in addition to the spare change, offered to share their meals and more than once, a warm bed. This was my life for the next 3 months.

St. Boniface was home to the Youth Hostel, housed in what looked like an old castle. There was a statue of Louis Riel out front. I would visit there weekly to catch up and trade some road stories. I was getting so comfortable at Holley and Lucy's that I was beginning to wonder if I would stay there, forever content and totally domesticated. I had to make a move. So one morning I broke the news and said an almost regrettable goodbye. I set out to finish what I started.

> ...*I started feeling like a runaway,*
> *Every time I went downtown,*
> *Yeah, Holley and Lucy, they had me,*
> *I was seventeen and nailed right down...*

HOLLEY -2000 – FROM THE ALBUM - GIRLS

I truly loved those girls, and though I never saw them again I'm certain they eventually managed to fulfill their dreams on the strength of their will alone.

SASKATCHEWAN

Not much ever happened for me in Saskatchewan. It was what I envisioned a lost soul would experience in Limbo. Stuck right in the middle of the desolate prairies, as flat as a wedge of two dimensional pie, somewhere between where I was going to or coming from. I'm sure there are some interesting people there like anywhere else, but I never found much of an excuse to linger.

My previous ride had dropped me at a deserted crossroad heading North as far as I could tell. That's when a well groomed young couple with two young kids picked me up. They were from Saskatoon and were taking the kids to the lake. Lake Diefenbaker to be exact. A body of water so saturated with salt that apparently you float like a cork in it. A popular Saskatchewan attraction. The folks had that conservative look that suggested they may hold membership in some clean cut cult.

"Mom, is this guy a hippie?", one of the kids asks.

"Yes Timmy, he's a hippie, be nice.", says the mother.

I'm thinking to myself, "I've made it! They think I'm a hippie!"

The kids were cautious at first, nervously giggling and feeding the hippie their peanut butter and jelly sandwiches, snatching back their tiny hands like they were feeding a bear in a cage.

Off in the distance we noticed an obstruction on the road miles ahead. It was too small to make out exactly what it was. Five minutes later we were close enough to see that it was a Ford Pinto. It was in the middle of the road on its roof, lazily spinning in circles like a playground merry-go-round. The father stopped a safe distance from the wreck.

"C'mon, let go see if we can help", he says to me as we cautiously approached the metallic carousel.

We could now see crumpled bodies inside the car and were preparing for the worst.

"Oh, Jeezzz", says the father.

As we crept closer, we could make out what sounded like laughter and increasingly louder music. It became apparent by the whoopin' and hollerin' coming from inside the car that no one was injured. 'Life is a Carnival' by The Band blared through the car speakers. Quentin Tarantino would have been inspired. The squeaky door slowly opens...

Three guys and two girls spill out of the car, laughing, and in between gulps of air, apologizing for blocking the road. The guys all had long hair and didn't appear to be much older than me. One of them was obviously trying unsuccessfully to grow his first beard. The girls were both pretty. Dressed in blue jeans, they wore tye died t-shirts over their braless curves. The driver told me they had become bored with the straight road and started weaving the car back and forth with the music just before they ended up in their present position. The guy, still laughing, told us with the certainty of a musician that the roof hit the pavement on a perfect downbeat. With our help, the six of us managed to flip the car back over. They thanked us profusely and slowly drove away. We just stood there staring in awe as the music and laughter slowly faded into the flat landscape. This was my first trip through Saskatchewan. I can't make this shit up.

The oldest sister, Diane, has married and left another vacancy in the old school. The younger siblings have new found freedom. They do not seem to be affected by the absence of their older brother and sister and continue on, as children will.

Young Susan has constructed a small caged shelter at the base of the walnut tree where she tends to her two rabbits. Tina follows her around tirelessly, doing her best to help out. I have grown bored with this humdrum voyeurism and attempt to broaden my range. In my limited capacity, I try to make contact with the Boy by using the big maple as a giant beacon and receiver, but unlike Nicola Tesla, I am sadly unsuccessful. It seems I can do nothing more than hope and wait as his mother Rita does...

NORTHERN ALBERTA

I knew Vancouver was not going anywhere and as long as I was headed in the general direction I was content, but most times I would go wherever the driver was headed if the company was good. It was not necessarily a straight line to the West Coast.

I was now in Northern Saskatchewan on the Yellow Head Highway and after a series of rides from tiny town to tiny town, I ended up much further northwest in the city of Grande Prairie, Alberta. This was long before the oil boom and Grande Prairie was not yet so grand. A fellow traveler had invited me to crash at his big brother's place. Out here on the road, when you run into someone familiar, even if you only shared one fleeting conversation, it's like a family reunion. We had met on one of my visits to the hostel in St. Boniface when I was staying with Holley and Lucy.

Big brother was kind of strange. He had an underground radio show at the local station and presented himself as a Dracula type character, Baron Von something or other, not unlike Count Floyd from SCTV. Tall, thin and pale, he had a cape with a high collar, a coffin bed and a fantastic record collection. His musical taste was eclectic, bands like Captain Beefheart and Wild Man Fischer with a spattering of English groups like Audience and The Kinks. I spent hours pouring through his milk crates full of records, most of which you would never hear on mainstream radio.

Milk crates were the 'Ikea Furniture' of the 70's. You could find them piled up behind most grocery stores. Back when a quart was still a quart, record albums fit into them perfectly. You could lay boards across them for shelving or use them to elevate your bed. Perfection in modular design and a requirement for anyone under twentyfive in their first apartment.

The brothers talked politics way too much for my liking. The 'Baron' fancied himself to be a political activist, maybe even a Communist. Likely the only one in a town where nobody really seemed to care. On occasion, when their heated discussions got louder than the music, I would wander downtown alone. I have never subscribed to politics or organized religion. My years spent growing up in the Catholic school system were more as a passive observer than as a devoted follower and my politics echoed the same sentiment. The Golden Rule sums the whole picture up for me, without any hidden agenda or material gain. Amen.

Having long hair in the early 70's made you instantly approachable by other 'longhairs'. It would start off by flashing the mandatory peace sign, then, "Hey brother, are you new to in town?" and after some more small talk about music, straight into, "Would you like a toke?" Before you knew it you had entered the elite brotherhood of the local cast offs and undesirables that every small town clergyman feared.

HECKS ANGELS

The local motorcycle gang in Grande Prairie rode 400 Hondas exclusively. They were small town kids as green as me, just trying to make sense of it all. Hippies on scooters. Most of them were dressed in Army Surplus jackets and boots, their jackets adorned with Grateful Dead patches and peace symbols. Seeing my battered guitar and without ever hearing me play, I was instantly invited to entertain at all of their frequent parties. There wasn't a lot of desirable entertainment in town other than once in a while when someone would put together a dance at the local Legion. Just walking into a room with a guitar back then could catapult you into instant popularity. My trusty instrument, once again had provided admission.

The gang ran the local drug trade which consisted of mostly pot, hash and LSD. In this small town there really wasn't much of a clientele. It existed for convenience more than profit. Sales were mostly conducted within the group. This was the most passive bunch of 'bikers' I have ever encountered. Everyone in town knew them and what they did.

It felt like I could have casually asked a mailman, "Excuse me sir, I'm new in town. Would you know where I might score some illegal drugs?"

"Sure thing! Just look for a fella on one of those 400 Honda's. He'll fix you up", would be his cheerful reply.

"Thank you sir! Have a nice day!"

They had sales incentives and daily specials. Each purchase was rewarded with free ZigZag papers or a pipe, and for the LSD users, day-glow posters. If you bought in quantity they would throw in the black light lamp. 'Please and Thank You' drug dealers and all around, a respectable bunch of nice guys.

My limited geographical restrictions sometimes cause me to despair. I long to travel. The Boy is no doubt fulfilling his curiosity. I am anxious for his return to fulfill mine. I follow the roots and arteries of the ancient maple up and over the rooftops to the uppermost branches. From here I see the endless fields that have replaced the once dense forest. The modern motor cars on the paved road out front seem to move over the horizon and out of my vision as fast as light...

THE SUMMER SOLSTICE

The gang had invited me to their annual 'bush party' on the Summer Solstice. I brought my guitar and my backpack with me because I was told the party could last for days. They don't have much going for them when it comes to trees in Grande Prairie. It was more like a shrubbery farm than a forest, the largest bushes being maybe 10 feet high, spindly and spaced far apart. Not ideal cover but a party is a party. There were two kegs of beer, plenty of smoke, forty to fifty people and lots of LSD. Giddy up!

On the longest day of the year this far North, the sun doesn't set completely, it just kind of quickly dips below the horizon for a few minutes then starts coming right back up a few inches over like some kind of cosmic peace sign. It's like time folds into itself from one day to the next with nothing in between. I suspected Captain Kirk and Spock may have experienced their first 'worm hole' encounter here.

The kegs were tapped, the drugs dispensed and the party was well under way. It was a great mix of people. The bikers, their hippie student friends home for the summer and small town country girls of all shapes and sizes. As the day *or* night wore on and the cornucopia of drugs and alcohol took effect, everything started to accelerate.

The bikers had rigged up a microphone and some speakers to couple car batteries and my makeshift stage was on the tailgate of a '66 Chevy pickup. With a hit of LSD ingested and a beer in hand I was hovering in that transitional place just before you become aware of how wasted you're getting. With the pleasant buzz tickling my molecules, there couldn't have be a better time to start singing.

I was half way through the third song when one of those magical doors in my head opened wide. It seemed suddenly that I understood the meaning of everything. Awesome! The crowd was under my spell or too stoned to do anything else, so in addition to the music I began spouting words of wisdom in between songs, like a shaman or an oracle or maybe more like Yoda. Really vague 'meme' stuff and they were buying it with wide eyed wonderment.

I would say something like, "Seek the truth and you will find it", and everyone would ooh and awe and nod their heads. This was fun!

"The proof is in the puddin'"

Whoaa! I was on a roll!

Remembering what my old carny friend from Northern Ontario had told me...

"When you get a crowd under your spell, kid, the best thing to do is to pull a 'Snagglepuss' and exit stage left before your hold starts to weaken. Say your bit and split."

It was time for my curtain call. After what seemed like hours or days, the worm hole thing, I announced to my new found followers, "I have been called upon to continue my quest into the unknown."

Someone at the back of the crowd shouted, "Far out, man!"

The group took up a collection and I gratefully accepted some much needed traveling money. My pack and guitar were distributed onto separate motorcycles and the entire bike gang escorted me to the outer edge of town. I was seated behind the guy on the lead bike, my arms extended, my long hair blowing in the wind. It was surely an 'Easy Rider' moment, like Jack Nicholson without the football helmet.

As part of a long goodbye ceremony I was presented another offering for the journey. A case of Pilsner and a 1/4 ounce of Blond Lebanese Hashish for the road. I watched as they turned around and faded into the distance to return to the bush party. It was a beautiful day, or was it night? I was still very gloriously high. Could life get any better? I was about to find out.

THE REZ

So here I am in this Northern Alberta wonderland, heading south out of Grande Prairie. The Honda parade is long gone by now and the party goers are likely tapping into the second keg, listening to "Born To Be Wild" on somebodies 8 track. Off in the distance I see a little blue Mazda pickup truck approaching through the heat ripples coming off the tarmac like a desert mirage. The tiny cab appears to be packed, the springs are sagging. I'm not expecting a ride. The small truck began slowing down long before they got to me and glided over, crunching into the gravel at my feet. Inside were three large native guys, about six hundred collective pounds of muscle, blubber and long straight black hair. The guy on my side says, "Throw your stuff in the back and hop in". I assumed they wanted me in the back but they insisted I squeeze into the front with them. It was impossibly tight and uncomfortably intimate, but somehow I fit in. They said they would take me to the main road into Edmonton (The Yellow Head), but they had to make a stop at the 'Rez' first. I was happy to be on the move. The guys, having noticed my beer explained that we were on a 'Dry Rez', but not to worry, there would be no trouble, "we'll just keep the box covered up", the driver said with a knowing wink. After a few turns down the red dirt back roads I had become totally disoriented. Finally, they pulled into an old weather beaten clapboard farm house with a collection of equally well worn cars and pickups parked around it in the neighboring field. The springs groaned with relief as we spilled out of the little Mazda.

Inside, the house was rockin'. It was set up like an old western saloon, complete with a long, mirrored bar. My new friends found a table and bought me a beer as we settled in.

"Why don't you play us a few songs?" one of them asked.

I couldn't refuse, they had already unplugged the old Seeburg jukebox in the corner. I played every song I knew, twice, and even threw in a couple old Hank Williams songs for good measure. Three hours later after many more beers and a good meal generously provided 'on the house' by the bar keep, we squeezed back into the mournful blue truck and were on our way.

At the main highway, after goodbyes were exchanged. I unloaded my pack, my guitar and my beer.

"Wait a minute", the driver said, "Thanks for the tunes. Here's a case of beer for being a good sport"

Pulling a u-turn in their tin chariot, they floated off into the same mirage in which they had earlier appeared. I stood there grinning and shaking my head, loaded down with beer and wondering if parting gifts were a tradition in Northern Alberta.

Reviewing this memoir of the Native people reminds me of my 20 day journey from Halifax to Montreal when I first arrived in the new world. A group of us are setting out in a covered wagon, pulled by a team of muscular horses. Our guide, on horseback is an Iroquois Indian. He regards me with quiet curiosity and respect. The gentleman at the reigns of the team smells of whiskey and fermented ale. My fellow passengers are filled with nervous excitement having finally arrived in the New World. After a long day, we finally make camp in a small clearing by a peaceful, lazy river.

The Indian guide is very friendly and intrigued with my bonnet. Using a mixture of broken French and exaggerated hand gestures he offers a trade. My bonnet for a pair of rabbit skin gloves....

THE TRAILER

I had been dropped off at a secluded intersection, in the middle of a nowhere I've become familiar with. There is an abundance of 'nowhere' out here in the prairies. The last remnants of the LSD was still teasing my nerve endings, I was kinda drunk, with 2 cases of beer, a quarter ounce of hash, a guitar and a backpack in my possession. It was getting late in the day. There was not a house or a gas station in sight. The only shelter within miles was an old abandoned construction trailer set back from the road. The hippie bikers had warned me to watch myself out here as I got closer to Southern Alberta because there were many rednecks and bad cops who didn't take kindly to us 'longhairs'. Naturally, I got a little paranoid and decided my best plan of attack would be to bunk down in the trailer and maybe leave behind some of my parting gifts. Besides, the beer was heavy and hard to carry, even though a case of beer in Western Canada is only 12 bottles.

I had traveled south far enough for the idea of night time to be back into the equation. It was dusk and I stumbled through the broken door of the musty, windowless trailer into total darkness. Just as I had cleared a spot and was settling in I heard a voice,

"Who goes there! This is my spot, motherfucker!"

Just short of pissing my pants I managed to squeak out, "Just a little ol' songwriter with a guitar and a case of beer".

There was silence, then a snicker, "Well make yourself at home friend. You just scared the crap out of me too. You're welcomed to stay as long as you don't mind the smell, snicker snicker."

As it turned out he was just another guy from the Rez heading to Edmonton to visit his brother, currently in rehab. He knew the guys that had dropped me off and the bartender from the speakeasy. We stayed up late, exchanged stories, drank a bunch of the beer, smoked some hash and sang old country songs in the dark until finally crashing.

In the morning he was gone like a ghost. I never even got a good look at him but according to my phantom friend, Calgary was definitely a place to avoid if you were native or had long hair. There was a construction boom going on. The roughnecks it attracted were the kind that thought a good way to blow off some steam was to get into a fist fight or even better to catch a hippie, teach him a lesson and cut off his hair. Scalping – A Western Tradition. This sounded like a place I would rather avoid so I changed my intended route and continued on my way due west into the Rockies.

ROCKY MOUNTAIN WAY

I'm sure many of you have may have seen pictures of the Rocky Mountains in books or on TV, but unless you see them in the flesh you can't possibly have any idea how absolutely mind blowing they really are. It was certainly a glorious sight after witnessing the dirty brown haze that hangs over Edmonton. Luckily, I got a ride straight through that rusty dome and into the clear blue skies of Jasper National Park.

Leaving the prairies is not as abrupt as entering them from the East. There are miles of badlands, rolling foothills, picture perfect farms and wild horses. This was the landscape of the Cowboy shows I grew up with on black and white TV. The panoramic, technicolor version being much better.

Seeing the mountains off in the distance was surreal. At first they just looked like a heat ripple or a lake shimmering on the horizon but as I got closer they began to take shape. Their deceptive size kept increasing, and by the time I actually got right into them, I could not help but be in awe as to how immense they really were. They rose majestically above the summer heat, disappearing through the clouds into an impossible snowy atmosphere. The fragrance of surrounding pine and cedar trees that climb into the heavens permeate the senses. After months on the dry, desolate prairies, it surely had a positive impact on the senses

There was a great youth hostel at my first stop in Jasper. It was made up mostly of big army tents with bunks, set back from the road in the Alpine forest. The people running the hostel were local kids who were grateful they didn't have to leave this wonderland for a summer job. Thank you Pierre ET.

I still had most of my stash with me, which was impossible to conceal, but I couldn't convince myself to leave my 'gifts' in the construction trailer. I knew this was not really a wise decision. I had been stopped and searched before in Northern Ontario (Thunder Bay to be exact) and it was not a pleasant encounter. The cops just dumped all my possessions on the roadside, filtered through my dirty laundry and left me to collect the mess, with orders to be gone by the time they returned. Bastards!

So – sitting around a campfire with a mismatched group of strangers I announced, "I've got a case of beer and some hash. Does anybody have a pipe and a bottle opener?"

Silence, then on mass almost everybody ran to their assigned tents and came back with every kind of dope smoking paraphernalia known to man. We tried our best to burn it all but eventually you're as high as you can get. We sat there sipping beer, stoned and content in our surroundings. I recall the equally intoxicating mountain air and the stillness in the camp which was only enhanced by the crackle of the fire. I was too high to play my guitar or even talk for that matter.

There was about eight to ten of us; a young couple from Australia, a few German students, and the rest of us from various parts of the country. We were all gloriously chewed.

To our left we suddenly heard a racket in the bush. Whatever it was, it was BIG! I'm sizing up my new companions. If it's a Grizzley, I was pretty sure I could outrun a good number of them. Lucky for the slow ones, it wasn't a bear. To our disbelief, a glorious Elk buck muscled its way straight into the opening! It was enormous, sporting a rack of disproportionate antlers that were supported by a muscular, powerful neck. It stood no more than thirty feet from us. It didn't seem concerned. We were the trespassers, if anything, it looked a bit annoyed with our presence. I don't know if we were all just overwhelmed or paralyzed in a smokey dream, but no one made a peep. Jaws were agape. Eyes were-a-poppin'! After what seemed like eternity the Elk calmly turned away, strutted back into the brush and disappeared. It was the most graceful exit I have ever witnessed. No one spoke. All we could do was grin stupidly at each other, perhaps knowing we had just shared something unbelievable.

There was no way anyone could trump what had just happened. One by one we retreated to our canvas shelters. I'm sure I wasn't the only one laying on my bunk replaying the whole scenario. In my slumber, I fantasized that it had been a talking Elk, sounding suspiciously like Mr. Ed, The Talking Horse. "Hello Wilber!" What a night! All in the company of strangers. I drifted off in mid-chuckle.

The next morning I had slept in. By the time I got to the highway there was already a long formation of hikers stretched out in front of me.

Hitchhiking etiquette dictates that you leave ample space between participants and proceed to a respectable distance from the last in line. In this case it was about a mile and a half. On the way, I was reunited with each of my recently initiated campfire brothers and sisters. One by one, seeing as I still had a bit of hash to get rid of, I reasoned with myself that the best way to dispose of it would be with their generous help. So, as I proceeded down the line I had a morning toot with each of my fellow travelers. By the time I got to my designated position at the end of the line, I was so high I just laid there in the long grass at the side of the road and had a wonderful dreamless nap.

When I woke up everyone was gone. It was getting dark again. I had no choice but to head back to the hostel for another night. Knowing my illegal stash was finally gone had restored my calm and I played my guitar enthusiastically for the new arrivals before turning in. I half anticipated a repeat performance from the elk but it was destined to be a one time engagement.

The Boy, now a man, dreams about this series of events after having put pen to paper and I also witness the marvel. I am convinced he must be exaggerating as older men are want to do. Could mountains really be this big? Could lakes really be this shade of blue? Although amused, I am certain that talking elk do not exist, let alone a talking horse.

I feel fortunate to witness this alien landscape if only through the eyes and mind of the Boy. The topographical map in my first classroom barely registered anything between Upper Canada and Vancouver...

BANFF

The road south weaves lazily through the valley's between the mountain ranges from Jasper to Banff National Park. Most of the drivers on this stretch are tourists with kids. Not normally the ideal type of traveler that would desire to pick up hitch hikers. It isn't Wawa, but it likely holds a close second for the difficulty of getting a ride. The exotic landscape is so distracting it really doesn't matter if you get picked up or not. When it finally does happen, you have to stick your head out of the open window to see the mountain peaks. This practice makes it very easy to pick out the other first timers. The countless lakes are improbable, unique shades of blue or green. Giant big horn sheep, bears and elk feed lazily on the roadside, seemingly posing for the tourists that pull over with their cameras in hand. I'm sure in some language or culture, there may be an appropriate expression that describes the feeling of wonder I had, but it's not in my vocabulary. The best I could come up with was "Holeeee Fuuuuck!"

Way down in the picturesque valley ahead, I spotted what would be my next stop.

The youth hostel in Banff Park was in a mountain chalet parked on a ledge overlooking the pristine Lake Louise. Out on the patio, you got a view of both the lake, and off in the distance, the world famous Banff Springs Hotel. This hostel could have been a five star resort. I assumed that maybe someone had given me the wrong directions but this was really it. The place was crawling with people. A tour bus full of Japanese High School kids and their chaperons had just arrived. I settled in and after a shower and a meal, played a little impromptu concert for them. They listened politely and when I played a few Bob Dylan songs, they softly sang along.

When I was done, I offered my guitar to anyone who wanted to play a song. There were a few excellent players in the bunch. They sang 'Beatle' songs, with an accent, "Brackbuud singin' in duh dead of nigh!" No one spoke much English, but it didn't matter. We sang, we laughed. One of the chaperons did a Jerry

Lewis style stand up routine that was hilarious, even though I didn't understand a word. I'm guessing, laughter is contagious in any language.

I went to sleep that night pleased to be a part of this friendly planet.

Rita has received a post card from the Boy. The photograph on the front is of a wondrous, castle like hotel on a brilliant blue/green lake and reads, "Greetings From Lake Louise." She sits at the kitchen table, studies it and smiles, perhaps longing for a taste of adventure as much as I. He writes that he is well and offers barely enough information to fill the space on the small card. Rita turns up the radio and cheerfully continues her housework...

I spend the afternoon listening to a conversation between the Boys younger sisters. Susan is talking to her little sister, as young girls do, about boys. Susan has never kissed a boy and very much wants to, but she is worried she does not know how to do it right. Her little sister Tina generously offers to be the test subject...

OGO POGO

The next few days took me across a few more mountain ranges and down an endless slope into the Okanagon Valley. It was just after dark and from the crest as we began our descent into the valley, the lights in the town below twinkled as if the sky had been turned upside down.

In the middle of this parched landscape is a large cerulean blue lake with it's own version of the Loch Ness Monster, the dreaded Ogo Pogo. On the southern shore is the town of Kelowna, on the northern shore, Penticton. They are connected by a floating bridge that cuts the lake in two. The local fruit farmers visit the hostel there looking for anyone who may want work for a few days. I took advantage of this opportunity and made myself some traveling money doing odd jobs for a week at one of the many local wineries. I used my new found prosperity to buy new guitar strings, some road supplies and a proper sit down meal. My original 65 dollars had disappeared months ago and the generous donations from my Alberta biker friends had dwindled down to a few dollars. After a much needed visit to the local laundromat, I was literally ready for a clean start. The coast was calling and I was nearing what I thought was my final destination. Next stop Vancouver!

...Into my early adulthood, I believed in earnest that these mythical sea creatures actually existed. Ancient boat devouring monsters and fre breathing dragons would regularly invade my dreams and rob me of sleep until the wee hours. The elders in my village also attested to their existence and told frightening tales of their personal encounters by candle light...

VAN

Wedged between the mountains and the Pacific Ocean, Vancouver appears to be sheltered from the rest of the country and the world. The population is made up of a universal mish-mash of colliding cultures. Other than good old Lake Diefenbaker in Saskachewan, I had never seen salt water before and the mighty Pacific was far more impressive than that little prairie pickle barrel.

The hostel in Vancouver was in an old abandoned army barracks on Jericho Beach, not far from Simon Fraser University. There were many reunions with my fellow roadies. Some had already been here for weeks.

When you run into a kid you may have met a

month ago in Northern Ontario, the transformation is quite remarkable. I guess road wisdom tends to accelerate the growing process. We were no longer the 'green' kids that started out. Everyone of us had experienced some kind of life changing revelation to get us to this point. Some good, some bad. Although we were not fully ripened yet, our time away from the tree had earned us a tiny slice of maturity.

Gastown was an exciting place for me. It was not unlike going to the circus when I was a kid. People selling watches and jewelry from displays on the inside of their jackets, the barkers in front of the Wax Museum urging the tourists to enter, artists and buskers line the street, performing everything from gorilla theater to juggling acts, pretzel like contortionists and of course lots of street singers. They welcomed newbies like myself with gratitude and respect. I managed to earn decent money with ease and soon discovered, due to the city's mild climate that some people actually did this year round. One guy on the strip had an act that culminated in a death defying leap over a box of wooden matches. Brilliant! The anticipation building up to the actual jump was as nail biting as any Evil Knievel stunt. He actually made a comfortable living at it!

There were two crusty old timers on the street that all the regulars seemed to know and love. They would park their chairs outside of this old bar on Georgia Strait and play a few old country songs, collect their change and retire inside to drink until the money was gone. As the day went on and the drinks took their toll, they would argue about what to play next. The arguments were almost as entertaining as the music. Somebody on the sidewalk would shout out a request...

"I never wanna play that fuckin' song again!" the old timer would grumble to the crowd and to his playing partner.

The other old guy would snicker and go right into the song with everything he had...

"Put your sweet lips, a little closer, to the phoooone!..."

Sometimes it escalated into a full out fist fight between the two of them. Legend was, they had been doing this for over 20 years.

It was rare to meet anyone who was actually from Vancouver, especially in Gastown. The people that really lived in the city didn't hang out much in this part of town. This was a global village, populated by tourists and transients. I really wanted to immerse myself in the local culture but aside from a few natives there wasn't a specific culture to define.

Gastown was mostly just a bunch of implants from somewhere else or sight seers just passing through. It was apparent there just had to be a local music scene happening somewhere, but it was so far under the surface that I found it impossible to access it in the short time I spent there.

On occasion, I would cross paths with an old acquaintance from Rochdale College in Toronto. 'Sneaky Pete' had been one of the legendary chemists during it's notorious hay days. It appeared that he may have self-tested a bad batch of his bathtub LSD. He wandered around talking to himself and his old dog. In his ratty old suit, he reminded me a lot of Tom Waits. Everyone avoided him.

I would share a bench with him outside of the hostel on occasion and take care of his surprisingly conversational dog while he went in to get a meal and clean up. The dog was a Shepherd cross and every bit as gnarly and worn out looking as Pete. Sneaky told me he had come to Vancouver to reunite with his runaway daughter. I sincerely hoped his story would have a happy ending. He was a good person.. Hell, even his dog knew that.

118

ON THE BEACH

I was introduced to Wreck Beach by a native Vancouverite of Japanese decent. Jasmine worked at the hostel. I was told you could camp on the beach for the summer if you got tired of staying at the old barracks or got kicked out. Hostelers were only allowed a bed for four days at a stretch. Most people would just sleep on the beach for a few nights and then return to re-register.

Stairs made of old logs were cut into the sandy cliffs from the beach to the university campus on top. It was a popular spot for both students and teachers alike. It turns out, being declared a Free Beach also meant that no clothing was required and almost everyone took advantage of this freedom. I had never seen so much naked flesh before or since.

The beach was covered with large cedar logs that occasionally would be liberated from a log boom on route to a sawmill on the Georgia Strait. Too big and heavy to remove, they were arranged into orderly rows to provide shade and privacy for the sunbathers.

While I was getting accustomed to the scenery, to my delight, my shapely guide had removed all her clothing as was the custom. Good God, she was perfect! An Oriental Goddess no doubt. Every curve of her body was as if it had been sculpted by one of the Masters. Not a tan line, a bronze idol come to life!

Grinning slyly, she whispered, "well, aren't you going to take off your clothes?"

I stuttered, "Y-Yeah sh-sure." and tossed my clothes off in an enthusiastic stupor, trying my very best not to look intimidated.

I couldn't believe this was happening. I wondered what the guys at home would say when I told them this one. This was way better than seeing my grade school teachers bare boob!

"Oh yeah" she said, " you should put that away. This

is a public place, you know."

I looked to where she was pointing.

"Oh shit!" I had an erection! "Sorry. sorry" I exclaimed and as nonchalantly as possible, dug a small hole and made myself comfortable in the sand. Face down, of course.

Jasmine produced a beach towel for us to share but I opted to keep things contained in my makeshift sand tunnel. And there I stayed. Every time I thought my control was finally returning she would shift into another pose and yet another magnificent landscape would reveal itself. My poor white country ass had never been exposed to the sun's harmful rays before. It fried lobster red in about two hours. "Jeezzus!"

I ended up camping at Wreck Beach for a good part of that summer. Long enough to become desensitized to the nudity. After a while, the people that came by with their clothes on were the weirdos and were regarded with righteous disgust.

It had taken me 4 and a half months to reach this oceanic paradise, free from the burden of work, school and even clothes for that matter. After about nine weeks the novelty started to wear off. Catholic guilt, perhaps. In a moment of clarity, I realized my journey didn't necessarily have to come to an end.

There was a lot more undiscovered country hidden from the casual tourist. It was time for my crimson derriere to hit the highway. I could wind my way back to tobacco country, recharge my finances and reunite with the many friends I had made on the way.

For the next 2 years I never stayed much more than a week in one place, except for tobacco harvest. I was a cross-country couch surfer and it was a happy time. I explored countless small towns off the beaten path to the north and south of the Trans Canada Highway. Whenever I required more money, my guitar and a street corner would provide. Occasionally, someone would offer me a part time job for a few days. There was an endless supply of new people and places on the back roads and I intended to see and meet them all. I recall at the time wondering why anyone would want to travel to another country or continent when there was so much to experience right here in this promised land? I was determined to discover every square inch of it, and I drifted as far from The Trans Canada Highway and familiar territory as possible. Main roads are for tourists and billboards. The true fabric of this nation is neatly tucked away off the beaten path.

HEARTBREAK

On one of my trips home, I took yet another job in tobacco harvest. I had graduated to becoming a 'kiln hanger', the highest paid job on the farm. It was great for me, I wasn't bothered by heights and I could stick a radio up there and groove out all day in the shade. I treated the task as if it was a choreographed dance. James Brown on the radio, a soul spin and hang the stick. I rarely fell out.

I met a girl that summer, on a Saturday night at 'The Hall' in Delhi. Tommy James and The Shondells were headlining. They were playing 'Crystal Blue Persuasion' when I first saw her. She looked to be somewhere else. I held out my hand, bowed and asked for a dance. She accepted.

*The Boy is home for the summer. His mind,
once again preoccupied with a girl. I have
never been in love that I can recall and I
experience the thought of it through him. I am
not a stranger to affection, but it does not
compare to the all encompassing nature of this
beast. In his dreams, the emotion is most
pleasant and at the same time dangerously
distracting...*

Kim had just broken up with her boyfriend and we
ended up spending the rest of the night and most of
the summer together. I had bought an old Buick, and
Kim and I spent hours cruising the back roads of
Southern Ontario. I couldn't get enough of her. Five
foot two, eyes of blue. She was another song just
waiting to happen.

The normality of a relationship can put tethers on a
wandering soul. I had a desire to stick around for a
while. I was in love, or in retrospect, in love with the
idea of being in love. We were in my car on a little
excursion to Algonquin Park on the day that the
radio DJ sadly announced that Elvis Presley had
died. I thought about Mom and all those bad movies
we watched with her. It sparked a nostalgic desire to
remain in the safe predictability of a normal home.

By the end of harvest unfortunately, or in the big
picture perhaps fortunately, Kim had made up with

her old boyfriend. She said goodbye to me. Just like that. I was crushed. As crushed as a guy that has fallen in love with every girl he ever kissed could be.

As a songwriter, I heard it was important to write about what you know. She had given me the gift of a broken heart. An important thing to have in your arsenal when crafting a love song. Thanks Darlin'.

As luck would have it, broken hearts don't take a long time to heal when you're seventeen. The pain morphs into melancholy and eventually what's left is just a fond memory. Traveling cures everything. Traveling alone gives you license to re-tool and re-invent.

...And like a Southern Ontario Sunset,
She burns in the back of my mind,
Though summer has gone,
She's still the one,
I think about, all of the time...

SOUTHERN ONTARIO SUNSET -2006- FROM THE ALBUM-
PLAIN AND SIMPLE

MONTREAL FOG

The end of harvest is always a celebration in tobacco country. The harvest party is an alcohol drenched release usually held in the bunkhouse or in the farmers back yard. The cool autumn air is filled with music and laughter from Burford to Simcoe to Delhi, Tilsonburg, Langton and all the small tobacco towns along Lake Erie. Fifty plus consecutive days of enduring the August heat and the icy wet mornings of September requires a controlled environment to unleash the sleeping beast.

This year I had plenty of things to release. Besides making it through yet another season, Kim had just given me her devastating news. Even in the company of the inebriated tobacco gang I was alone in my misery. As the night progressed and the whiskey took hold, I searched for something more that would lift away this awful weight.

A clever plan was hatched by the end of the evening. Even in my youth I knew that drunken plans are usually best left forgotten. The next morning this one remained intact. Doug, the farmer's son and I would hop in my '69 Buick Le Sabre behemoth and go on a well deserved road trip. Three of our fellow workers were French guys from Montreal. Instead of dropping them off at the train station as arranged, we would drive them home. Road Trip!!

The harvest party is also where you usually collect your final paycheck for the season. It's a sizable lump of money. During the season there is not much time to spend your earnings, so aside from withdrawing a few small cash advances, you're left with the bulk of 5 or 6 weeks pay. The next day we loaded the car and the five of us headed for the Bank of Commerce in Burford to cash in. Having a pocketful of 20 and 50 dollar bills can make you feel like the king of the world. The thought of how long and hard you had to work for it disappears almost instantly.

Our next stop, Toronto and Rochdale College, the LSD Capital of Canada. Doug and I figured we could increase our earnings by purchasing a hundred hits from one of the resident chemists. The police were trying to evict everyone at the time. All the locks and door knobs had been removed from the rooms but the residents had refused to vacate and had their own home grown security force in place. We were assured that after following close instructions, we would soon be in our car, safe from the prying eyes of the police and 'the greenies', the not so hard to recognize RCMP agents that occupied the lobby and the streets around the building.

One hundred hits of acid, especially in blotter form is not very hard to conceal. The blotter was a measure of liquid LSD on a piece of paper, usually decorated with various symbols to indicate where the invisible drop was applied. This batch had yellow smiley faces. The package was easily concealed inside my shoe. After the purchase our chemist used his walkie talkie to communicate with their private security people in the building. Our skillfully coordinated escape proceeded down the service elevator to a unmarked door, through a large kitchen and out into an alley by the dumpsters behind the high rise. After a nervous but cautious casual walk down the back street to our car, we were home free. The French guys had been waiting patiently during the whole transaction. They didn't speak much English and I'm not sure they realized the intensity of our cloak-and-dagger caper. To celebrate, I pulled out the small package and distributed a hit to everyone in the car.

We would soon be out of this hellhole and on the open road. I chose to travel on Highway2, which was the old two lane Kings Highway that ran parallel to the busy 4-lane 401.

About a hour later we were almost beyond the city limits. Night had fallen, the street lights had turned on and I still wasn't feeling the desired effect of our purchase. I was beginning to suspect we had maybe been ripped off. I pulled over at a Mr. Submarine so everyone could grab something to eat for the road. We piled out of the car into the brightly lit store.

Florescent lighting is brutal when you're high, and this place had enough to light a room five times the size. One of the fixtures was flickering and buzzing like a hive of angry bees. The five us us got in line to place our order. I was last. Suddenly, like someone had flipped a switch in my head, "boinggggg!", the drug had unleashed its full power. I was suddenly desperate to get away from the hum of the lights. The guy taking orders at the till looked oddly like a sinister foreign interrogator and I had no desire to endure his questions. No longer hungry, I hastily removed myself and went back to the car. From the safety of my Detroit built fortress I could see the guys in there waiting patiently to place their orders. "Boingggg!", the drug took hold of Doug like someone had hit him on the head with a frying pan. He turned around to say something to me and realized I wasn't there. He also made a quiet,, wide eyed escape back to the car. Together, we watched as the LSD tsunami worked its way up the line. One at at time the rest of the crew were illuminated and took their leave. We left the parking lot, laughing hysterically, without any food.

Back on the road, we wove our way east through the small towns that scatter the north shore of Lake Ontario. The soundtrack for the journey was Rick Wakeman's 'Journey To The Centre Of The Earth'. There wasn't much chatter, except for the French guys who obviously couldn't follow the narration on the 8 track. There was a slight fog forming, likely because of our proximity to the lake, which enhanced the suspenseful story being told on the recording. I slowed down as the fog engulfed the car and made it difficult to see the road. I was so intrigued with the story that it took a while to realize that I was actually smelling smoke. In that instant I realized that the fog was not fog at all.

"There must be a forest fire happening near by. Do you smell smoke, Doug?"
He too was suddenly aware, "Yes, I do" he said.

When I was a kid, there was a small forest fire on our school bus route. This kind of appeared to be the same kind of scenario. Our bus driver, Mr. Poole had told us not to worry, "Cover your mouths and nose with your t-shirts kids and we'll be through the smoke in no time."

One of the older boys, bandanna in place like an old bank robber, walked in front of the bus to guide the driver when the smoke got too thick. We made it through without incident.

This time, Doug volunteered for the task. We had our windows up tight to keep the smoke out. Doug was outside on point, seemingly quite comfortable with his heroic calling. We had rolled along safely at walking speed for about five minutes when an enlightened Doug tapped on the window, "Hey, there's no smoke out here, man."

"Whaaaat!?!", I rolled the window down and caught a gulp of fresh air. "Shit!", it was us! We were on fire!

With Doug back in the car and our windows down I spotted a Red Barn Restaurant and swerved into the back parking lot. Coughing and choking, everyone piled out. The back seat was smoldering! One of the guys must have dropped a cigarette. Apparently, the smoldering upholstery in a '69 Buick after being marinated in tree shaped PineFresh has almost the same aroma burning timber. Doug and I unhooked the seat and hauled it out of the car into the parking lot. There was a burn hole around two inches in the upholstery and it was spreading. We tried to smother it but it had taken hold like a well lit cigar. We needed to douse it, and quickly. I sent everyone into the restaurant for water. It seemed to take forever as the hole increased in size and the smoke billowed out of the seat. They finally returned with orders of burgers and fries in addition to the large waters. "Jeezuss!" We doused the seat and aired out the car while we ate. The French guys in the back argued for a while, I assumed about who would sit on the wet spot. Nonetheless satisfied, we were back on the road, Rick Wakeman was still thundering through the speakers. No one had thought to change the tape.

Twelve long hours into our journey we entered the city of Montreal. Our buddies guided us in broken English through a series of crowded back streets to our destination. It was 10am. We had arrived at one of their homes. "You come eat now" our French friend insisted and the whole bleary eyed crew trudged into the small house.

It turns out our guy lived there with his girlfriend and his parents. As soon as we walked in the door his mother shouted with glee and gestured for us to sit at the kitchen table, bringing us coffee and biscuits, and all the while having cheerful animated conversation with her son.

On a tobacco farm there are two distinct groups, the 'table gang' and the 'primers'. The 'boat driver' remains neutral as he interacts with both groups. His job is to deliver the tobacco from the field to the table gang. I had worked on the same farm with these guys all summer and just then realized that I didn't really know any of their real names. Cleverly I came to the conclusion that this French Guy was Serge. That's what his mom kept calling him, after all. Then there was Patrick, the short one and Michel, the one with the afro. After our meal we all retired to the tiny living room. There was a squeal of delight as Serge's girlfriend entered the room. She had just gotten up and was wearing nothing but panties and a man's shirt. They embraced and started making out, apparently oblivious to us and the parents. Man, they were passionate. I tried not to stare.

Serge's Dad produced a big chunk of black hash and started knocking little chunks off of it. He pulled a device out of the drawer in the coffee table. I had never seen anything like it. It was a cigarette lighter, like the push in kind on the dash of a car, but it was built into a hand held ornate wooden box. The long, attached lamp cord was plugged into the wall and the small chrome button on the box, when pressed, illuminated the lighter. The hash was dropped onto the red hot devise and passed around. Push the button and instant hot knife! There should be one of these in every household. Think of all the charred kitchen knives it would save!

The next day, with a new selection of music on the 8 track, Doug and I started our return trip. 'House On The Hill' by Audience was the soundtrack. Of course the first leg of our get away had been such a success that we agreed it would be fitting to do more acid on the way back. We chose a random course for our return and soon got lost. Noticing one of those road signs with an airplane on it, I assumed there would be better directions at our disposal close to an airport. Soon the landscape was replaced by endless barbed wire fences and barren fields. Over to our left I spotted two Army tanks lumbering over the horizon. To our right, a group of solders in full battle gear were trudging across the sterile landscape...

"Holy shit Doug! I seriously don't think we're supposed to be here!", I said nervously.

Doug spotted a group of buildings up ahead. "We better pull in there and ask for directions." he suggested with a hint of hesitation.

You have to know that it's a guy thing, not to ask for directions, let alone in our present condition but this whole army thing was freaking me out and I desperately needed to get back into a more natural environment.

So, there we were, two long haired hippies, stoned on acid, pulling into an Army Base. It was kind of like a scene in a zombie movie. The solders milling about eyed us with curious amusement. I rolled down my window,

"Hey, how the fuck do we get outa here?", I asked one of them.

He looked into the car at us, laughed out loud and pointed to a guard shack at an exit gate about 500 feet ahead. After an interrogation by an extremely agitated MP with a crew cut, we were finally given directions to the nearest highway.

The next six hours of driving was pleasantly uneventful. The weight of my breakup with Kim had disappeared along with most of the effects of the acid by the time we entered Brant County. Back home in the safety of my room, I slept for twenty hours.

Seemingly exhausted, the Boy sleeps through the day. Remnants of the magical potion threaten to lure me into one of his hidden rooms. I am tempted, almost seduced. The Boy longs for intimacy. I am sympathetic, but I resist.

I am not estranged to intimacy, although my physical body was. In my present incarnation I experience a form of it every spring. The maple tree surges with a sweet nectar that races through the roots into the tips of the branches. Blood red buds form and fall as the new leaves take their place. This is likely a feeble comparison, but I imagine the exhilaration is similar.

Instead of succumbing to temptation, I use the opportunity to access his memories to see what I've missed. It is not unlike the theater, except in his present state much more colorful...

FROZEN IN TIME

It wasn't a long wait for my next impromptu adventure. Three months later I was spirited into a car at three in the morning and found myself back in motion. The destination was Trail, BC, just down the mountain from Nelson on the Columbia River. My friend Tom wanted to look up a girl we knew from home and asked me to come along for the ride. It was a hair-raising winter trip across the frigid northern shore of Lake Superior and through the black ice of the frozen prairies.

Tom was a truck driver. Not the knuckle dragging, Elvis lovin', chain on your wallet type. He was one hundred and fifty pounds of hip. Long straight blond hair and horn rimmed glasses, with a fondness for Rock 'n' Roll and all things intoxicating. He had left home with just the clothes he was wearing and a pocket full of credit cards.

We were in his orange '72 Toyota Tercel. When we got north of Sudbury, it got so cold we had to wedge cardboard in front of the radiator so we could get enough heat into the little tin bucket to keep the windows from frosting over. (an old truck driving trick.) We fearlessly drove one evening through a section of the Trans Canada Highway that was declared closed due to drifting snow. Our logic being, "If there's nobody else on the road, we can go straight up the middle, where there's less snow." It was a potentially dangerous decision and we could have easily ended up as two frozen 'hipcicles' found in a snowdrift the next day. Fueled with cocaine courage we plowed through, periodically stopping to examine a drift and how best to approach it to push through. In spite of the apparent danger it was a lot of fun.

In Saskatchewan I experienced 'black ice' for the first time. It was just that. It looked like dry asphalt and felt like it too, until you tried to brake. By the time we got into Alberta we were 'black ice veterans'. We remedied our prairie induced boredom by pulling brake jams at 50 miles an hour when there was no one coming and came up with a game. The objective was to see who could get the car to spin around the most times. Tom won that one, with twelve revolutions. I was reminded of the spinning car I had witnessed on my first Saskatchewan trip. The only difference being, we were right side up. I searched the tape case in the back seat for a copy of The Band's recording of 'Life is a Carnival.'

I was taking my turn driving when we got to the Salmo/Creston Pass which climbs over the Selkirk mountain range. It is something like 18 miles on a steep grade up and another 18 coming down. Near the top, the only way to stay on the road is to follow the fender high ruts in the slush and snow that the big trucks have left. Sheer cliff on one side and a wall of pure white snow carved out on the other. The road crews up there clear the path with massive snow blowers that shower waves of the white powder over the cliff into the canyon below. The continuous giant flakes fill in their path almost instantly.

When we reached the summit and started on our journey down the mountain there was a transport truck right on my ass and Tom casually commented, "Hey Bud, I think you better speed up."

I told him he was nuts, "Christ Tom! I can hardly hold it on the road as it is!"

Then he calmly explained that the truck behind us would gain momentum and not be able to brake safely on the downgrade. He pointed out the 'runaway ramps' that looked like they shot up on a forty five degree angle and ended abruptly at a dead end wall. "For the ones that get into trouble", Tom reported. I reluctantly sped up. Thank God the ruts were deep enough to keep us on the path and not take us over the edge into oblivion. It was a white knuckle ride all the way into the valley. I couldn't seem to gain an inch on the truck in my rear view mirror, which looked to be a breath away from pushing us into the abyss.

I have come to appreciate many more examples of Truck Driver's Wisdom over the years.

"Don't fuck with a truck on the mountain" is just one.

TRAIL

Trail BC is a small town, forty miles up and down a mountain from Nelson on the mighty Columbia River. The first person we ran into on the main drag was a friend from home. Bob Jackson had already settled in and had his own place. Bob was a scruffy looking guy from Simcoe, with long greasy black hair and a small scraggly beard. In spite of his unkempt appearance, he always had a wide friendly smile and a gentle kindness about him.

Tom had a wallet full of his Dad's credit cards, so we didn't have to worry about money. His family owned the large trucking company he drove for and they were cool with him spending their money. They apparently believed that a taste of the 'real world' would prepare him for when it was time for him to take over the family business. He eventually found his own apartment and I shared the place with Smilin' Bob. Bob played guitar too, an old twelve string Yamaha, and between the two of us we could entertain all night long. Our upstairs neighbor was a deaf guy, so there were never any noise complaints. Before you knew it, anyone having a party in town was inviting us over to play. Free food and drinks for us and an excellent way to meet new members of the opposite sex.

Trail was a mining town. Almost everyone had some kind of connection with the mine. If you didn't work for CoMinCo, your dad or brother did. The only exception was the few transient ski bums and us mostly jobless hippies. There were eight of us, and we eventually pooled together enough money to rent a large party house in Warfield, five miles up the mountain from Trail. Almost daily we would gather the beer empties from the night before, hop into this old Plymouth and coast down into Trail with the engine off. After cashing in our empties we would buy two dollars worth of gasoline for the drive home and meet the crew at the local diner for coffee and toast.

It was wintertime and Trail was a drab place with a different bar on every other block. The mighty Columbia River runs straight through the middle.

Down here in the valley the snow would turn into a dirty brown slush by noon. The mountains to the east and west of the valley allowed only 4 hours of sunlight onto the main street, from about 10am to 2pm. The rest of the day is spent in their shadow or preferably in a bar.

Our afternoons were spent at the Crown Point Hotel, drinking 25 cent draft until the place closed at 11pm. Five dollars would buy a round for the room and then you could drink 'for free' as everyone else took their turn. The regulars were a mix. Miners, miners' kids, the office girls and the young guys they attracted. The men's restroom had a condom dispenser with 25 cent colored condoms. Bar rules were, if you got a black one you won a free round of draft for the room. The lucky winners would blow them up and bounce them around the crowded room.

On your birthday, the custom was for every bar in town give you a free draft beer in a bedpan or a yard glass, a unique container for every bar. I never took advantage of this perc because, although I was never asked for I.D., I was still underage. (I guess that being a minor in a room full of miners can be easily overlooked.)

The Wurlitzer at The Crown seemed to always be playing Joe Walsh's "Rocky Mountain Way" or "The Joker" by Steve Miller. At 'last call' you could buy a box of beer, right at the bar to take home. That's when the party really started. A lot of these people were just getting off the afternoon shift and their night was just beginning. Bob and I, guitars in hand and beer in tow would linger outside near the parking lot nonchalantly waiting for the inevitable party invite.

ACID TEST

My world had two sets of Hollies and Lucies, the Winnipeg ones and the Trail ones. In this world, Lucy was my girlfriend and Holly was Smilin' Bob's. Holly was tall, dark and thin, but shapely. She was not named after a carburetor like my Winnipeg Holley was. Lucy was blond, blue eyed and shorter than me by a head. Her curved perfection was softened by a small layer of baby fat. We had met the girls at the Crown Point Hotel and got to know them at one of the frequent after parties. They both had grown up here. Miners kids.

When I say, she was my 'girlfriend', I mean we had sex. A lot. Looking back, I can't recall if our relationship was based on anything else, which was cool back then. Sex was not a complicated thing in the 70's. We mutually shared the comfort of our young bodies freely and without any real emotional expectation, perhaps knowing our practiced carnal skills may someday benefit a true love somewhere else down the line.

Lucy's older brother James claimed to be a graduate of Ken Kesey's 'Electric Kool-Aid Acid Test' and was devoted to carrying on Kesey's cosmic experiment. He thought of himself as an intellectual and always spoke in this academic 'I know better than you' voice. I was reminded of a few of my old school teachers. His library was filled with books on psychiatry and psychology, but whenever I saw him reading it was always Jonathon Livingston Seagull or Lord of The Rings. I thought of him as being a bit of a geek, except for one key deviation...

James had this little box full of pill bottles. Each one labeled with the type of LSD it contained as well as the vintage. He called it his 'Portable Travel Centre'. Geek or not, that was cool.

Occasionally he would enlist our group to be his test subjects. He documented everything and we were always up to the task. After all, it was like winning a free all inclusive vacation. I was the veteran, having first done acid at the age of thirteen, a most enthusiastic subject for this guys questionable, but extremely enjoyable little 'experiments'.

On one such occasion we were confined to a small room in his home, with food and drink, a stereo and the reel to reel tape recorder that he used to document the proceedings.

I often envision James as an old man, in a tattered lab coat, studying the contents of the tapes, tiny rec tangled wire rimmed glasses balanced on the end of his nose ferociously taking notes, his goblet of prune juice at the ready.

During this session, we were enjoying Frank Zappa's latest recording and I began laughing hysterically at some of the images the music was conjuring in my head. That guy *kills* me. I thought I was having a great time but the group became contaminated with the idea that I was 'freaking out'. Hell, I was just getting into the ride. I found the look of concern on their faces even more hilarious than Mr. Zappa, which started a chain reaction. Faster than you can say, 'Oh, Mama', I was doubled over on the floor laughing even harder. Lucy strategically perched herself on my chest playing nurse. Holly was desperately trying to find a record album that might mellow me out. Unconcerned, Smilin' Bob just chuckled and handed her a Todd Rundgren album, 'A Wizard, A True Star' and suddenly I was back on the rails. They gave each other a 'job well done look' and settled back.

> I didn't want to distress them further,
> but in my head,
> I imagined we had become a cartoon train.
> I was the engine, Bob, the coal car,
> Holly was the passenger coach
> and the lovely Lucy was the caboose.
> The back of the caboose was shaped like Lucy's
> perfect ass,
> bouncing up and down to the beat.
> We joyfully chugged through the next 50 minutes.
> I made them play "Onomatopoeia" twice.

Put that in your journal, professor!

One mild December morning, the four of us were squeezed into James' small car and driven to an old abandoned gold mine outside of town. I believe the LSD flavor of the day was 'Windowpane 69'. With kerosene torches in hand he led the us deep into the dark entrance instructing us to follow him in single file and not to stray. "After all, I don't want anyone falling down a mine shaft." The tunnel soon swallowed up all of the remaining daylight and the soft glow of the torches illuminated the rough wet walls. About twenty minutes later the torches began to run out of fuel, one by one. "Great plan Einstein" I thought to myself. I wondered if this was really part of the experiment. Then everything went black.

The color of true total darkness was astonishing and was enhanced by the constant drip-drip-drip of the stalactites. I felt like Jonah in stomach of the whale, still not certain if this had been part of the plan.

Our faithful guide instructed us to hold hands, stay on the rails and try not to panic, "I'm pretty sure I know the way out."

Pretty sure?! Where's that cartoon train when you need one?

One of the hands I held was cool and calm, I think it was Lucy's, the other one was Smilin' Bob's for sure. His were in a nervous sweat. I could feel the connection between all of us instantly like a soft electrical current. We struggled to balance ourselves on the slippery rail track, every now and again someone would slip off and splash into the ankle deep puddles on the mine floor. In the total darkness every sound was intensified and in my mind suddenly associated with a color. I imagined Professor James had assumed that our collective altered state would provide sufficient glow for a safe passage. It did not.

After what seemed like eternity we spotted a welcoming sliver of daylight coming from the entrance. An enormous wave of relief washed over the collective. I think, in spite of being stoned, all of

149

us, including me were getting a little worried.
Coming back into the light felt like being re-born.
The womb was cut deep inside the earth, the mine
tunnel, a birth canal. We were spit out one by one
into the blinding daylight. Quintuplets! I half
expected a giant boob milk dispenser to be waiting
for us when we got out into the open, like the one in
that Woody Allen movie. No one spoke a word until
we were safely deposited into the car.

Thus, ended our careers as lab rats.

GIRL TROUBLES

The girl Tom and I had come out to find somehow ended up staying at Smilin' Bob's place with me. There were only two beds. In the spirit of the era, Betty Anne and I shared a bed and each other. Lucy was cool with it. She usually spent the day times with me and on occasion I would stay at her place.

Tom had in the meantime, shacked up with this twenty something, ex-stripper named Ariel. She thought it was natural to wander around the apartment with nothing on but high heeled spikes. One afternoon, four of us guys were in Tom's kitchen playing cards and Ariel enters the room naked, except for her footwear and casually starts to do the dishes,

"You don't mind, do you boys? I haven't had a chance to do laundry and I just can't stand dirty dishes."

Her generous mound of pubic hair was long and black, and unaturally straight as a shoe brush. This display would totally disrupt the card game while we all gawked, but we still made a point of dropping by as much as possible. To this day I find playing cards rather boring without the exotic scenery.

One night, I had a vivid dream. I was at the good old Belgium Hall in Delhi and all my old friends were there. The 'Hall' was a 1500 seat room/bar in the centre of tobacco country. It played a crucial part in my musical development. Every Saturday, two Canadian bands would take the stage; Rush, April Wine, Fludd, Leigh Ashford, Max Webster, or anyone else that was making any noise on the Canadian airwaves. All for a $3.50 admission. In my dream, 'Bravebelt', with Randy Bachman and Fred Turner was performing. I witnessed the whole show in amazing detail. It crossed my mind that maybe it was a case of astral projection. I knew a girl downtown that swore by it. I wondered if it was possible to have an acid flashback in your sleep? Whatever it was, when I woke, I was undeniably home sick.

An early spring had arrived. I could no longer

control the traveling itch and decided to make the trek home to see family and friends to give them an update on my adventures.

Being on the road for me is like chocolate, I can usually never get enough, but this trip was driven by a homesick urgency. I wasted no time blowing through the still frigid Prairies in a day and Northern Ontario in two. Five days in total and I was on my mothers doorstep exchanging tearful greetings before sleeping off the trip in a familiar bed. It was great to be home in my old room with the smell of Mom's cooking wafting up the stairs, blended with the scent of Dad's cigarettes and port wine.

After a good rest, I caught up with the old crew in town. Although it seemed like I had experienced a lifetime of events, their lives seemed to be unchanged. I did not envy them.

I was told that 'Bravebelt' had actually played The Hall, while I was away. My friends described in detail the same concert that I had been to in my dream. Maybe there's something to this astral projection stuff after all. I felt an irresistible urge to get high. Not a problem. Even in the small town of Burford you could always find somebody that had some acid for sale so I scored some at a local hangout, Dot & Dave's Hole In The Wall' and got a lift home.

153

The Boy is home. It had been a long absence. Even though time holds no real significance to me, I am sometimes plagued by impatience. Quietly I slip into his dreams with the same ease as putting on an old pair of shoes. The powerful magic substance is also present and takes me by surprise.

Once again, I find myself transported into the finely furnished room. This time I find I am a girl seventeen and dressed in a simple Victorian gown. The door beckons for my attention. My curiosity is that of a girl of her age and I reach for the crystal glass doorknob, grasp it and fling it open. Instantly, without warning, I am sitting on the edge of the Boys bed! His eyes open, he sees me!

"Hi" *he says,* "Who are you?"

I am in shock. I feel he must not be made aware my true identity. He may not be ready. I panic for something to say. "M-M-Mary Force" I stutter.

The sound of my physical voice feels alien to me. Young Mary had been my 17 year old assistant before she passed. I must confess, my present incarnation had reminded me of her gentle soul and it was the first thing that came

154

to mind, under the circumstances.

"Where are you from?" *he asks.*

At this point in the conversation, I realize that the girl sitting on my bed couldn't possibly be real, but I figure, what the hell, I may as well go with it...

"Oh, I live out back in the graveyard." as if that wasn't anything out of the ordinary and after all, it was not entirely a lie.

" That's cool, I've seen your stone." *he replies casually.*

This was true. I don't believe I had ever spoken to a ghost before, but this one was pretty and her dress was like something out an old movie. She appeared to be more frightened of me than I was of her.

I believe I blushed, and as my cheeks burn, the spell is broken and I find myself feeling breathless and slightly embarrassed but back in the relative comfort of the maple tree...

She was gone, just as I had collected my wits and was preparing to ask her what I may expect to find on the other side... I closed my eyes and returned to the neon landscape inside my head but she was not there. By the morning I was convinced that she had been a by-product of my imagination.

Some of my friends were moving away to go to college, where I imagined they would get an eye opening taste of what life was really like. When you grow up out here, your world is very predictable and small. For the ones with plans to take over the family farm, school only served as a temporary escape from the inevitable. They all had wheels, mostly pickup trucks or muscle cars, part time jobs, monthly bills, and a structured idea of how they would fit into the impending future. For the first time I felt totally out of place. My future to date, had always been whatever happens tomorrow. I had never given much concern to what might be in the cards that far ahead.

I was 'reverse homesick' for Trail BC almost as soon as I got to Ontario. My life out there didn't require such looming responsibilities or commitments. Of course, it would be a good idea to make a bit of money before heading back out, so once again I turned to the tobacco fields for employment. There was always had a job waiting for me on any of the many farms I had worked on. I was a good employee and always stuck it out to the end. By toiling through spring planting and hoeing on a farm outside of Burford, I saved up a pretty good wad of cash over the next three or four weeks.

Somehow, my patience to do 'the in between' when traveling had disappeared. Maybe it was because I had concluded that my two favorite destinations were home and Trail. Another deciding factor was the fact that when I have money in my pocket I had an irresistible urge to spend it. A new kind of adventure perhaps. Something I had never done before. A scenic train ride sounded like it would be just the ticket.

At the time there were two Trans Canada Railway passenger lines. The Canadian Pacific and Canadian National. The CPR was the original route. I boarded that one, remembering one of Mom's favorite sayings when I was growing up that Dad "smoked like a CPR". Ticket in hand, I boarded at the little train station in nearby Woodstock.

I would recommend this trip to anyone. The stretch along Lake Superior is breathtaking. On some sections the track is precariously balanced on a rocky ledge with nothing but the icy water below. I played my guitar for drinks and tips in the club car during the long stretch through the Prairies. Down a few cars there was an observation car with two levels and a glass ceiling for sight seeing. At night time it was deserted and made for a great place to catch some sleep or just to stare at the stars streaking by. The tunnels into the Rockies and views down into the canyons are totally indescribable. If you've ever seen a picture in a travel brochure of a train in the mountains doing a figure eight through a tunnel like a mechanical snake with one end going in and the other coming out. This was the train. I rode it all the way to Vancouver and stayed a few days in the Jericho hostel before hitching back to Trail.

When I rolled into town everything had changed drastically. Betty Anne was pregnant and shacked up with my buddy Tom. His stripper friend, Ariel had moved back to Vancouver to resume her profession. Smilin' Bob had gotten kicked out of his place and was headed back to Simcoe for the tobacco harvest. He left in a $25 car he got at the local wrecking yard. At the time, you could put license plates on anything that rolled.

Almost overnight, mid-summer had arrived and everyone I was close to had decided to leave Trail, including Betty Anne and Tom. Holly and Lucy were nowhere to be found. They had checked out around the same time that I was on the train to Vancouver. The exodus to 'Anywhere But Here' was complete.

What I had thought of as my second home proved to just be a way station for most of my friends. I was the odd man out. This time being alone didn't feel so good. It seemed everyone I knew had some kind of plan for the future, even out here. Barely into my nineteenth year as ridiculous as it sounds, I decided it was time to grow up. Looking back I realize that this never really took hold. It was time again to turn to the only proven cure for all my problems. The open road. I would slingshot back to Ontario.

This time it was the CN train. It pretty much runs in a straight line across the country, running parallel with the Trans Canada. It was boring, but it gave me lots of time to think and plan about what to do when I got back home.

RE-INVENTING THE NORM

I landed a job in Brantford as soon I as returned and stayed with some friends from high school. I got a factory job making rubber nipples for Evenflow Baby Bottles. I guessed being 'the nipple guy' would have to do until I could get into Massey Ferguson's. That was where the big money union job was, manufacturing farm equipment. In the meantime I put my creativity to work to cure my boredom. I smuggled out sheets of nipples from the plant, two hundred nipples per sheet and covered an entire wall in my bedroom. It was a most impressive and functional installation and elicited many Freudian observations.

My next job was making grinding wheels at Bay State Abrasives. I found my own apartment, which was shared with one of my fellow workers. His name was Eric and he had what I've heard called, that crazy Peterborough look, slightly crossed, sky blue eyes, dirty blond hair and thin as a rail. He kind of reminded me of the weasel on the Deputy Dog cartoon show. We got moved in just in time to welcome Holly and Lucy from Trail. Somehow they had found me! For all the time I spent with them out west, it was only fitting to take them in.

Lucy hadn't lost her sexual appetite, and initially to my delight, every evening after our lovemaking, Holly would snuggle into the other side of the bed. We only had two beds and a quadraphonic stereo for furniture.

Holly had no interest in my room mate. Eric would listen to Tubular Bells by Mike Oldfield every evening and stare at us with this nutty look on his face. Holly said she was waiting for his head to spin around. Our cozy sleeping arrangement made for some long steamy, summer nights. I had a difficult time getting up for work every day, but how could I complain?

I worked the afternoon shift, five days a week and eventually the dynamic with the girls was becoming a bit of a strain. (wink wink). I had assumed they would get jobs and contribute in some way to our little love nest but they never got further than Victoria Park, downtown, where all the freaks hung out. I can't believe I'm saying this but the sex wasn't paying the rent and I was exhausted. Lucky for me, when they left Trail they had made a pact with each other not to put down any roots for a few years. They hung out for a month or so then pulled another disappearing act. I never saw them again and lost interest in the opposite sex for at least a week.

After I saved a bit of money I got an even better apartment to share with a few other guys. Doug and Kieth. Doug was the guy who came with me on the adventure to Montreal. Kieth was a hippie welder from Norwich that I had met a few years earlier. They had both secured jobs at Massey and were bringing home big pay cheques. We had the top floor of an old Victorian house. Three young girls our age lived downstairs.

It was a grand house on the West Street hill with a huge curved balcony and a big porch on the main floor. Before long we had befriended our fellow tenants. Eventually the back stairs that separated the two apartments remained unlocked and the entire house was shared. Everyone had a job and money to blow. It was one big happy family, just like in Trail. A great big old frat house and to my old country buddies, Brantford was the big city and the house was full of visitors every weekend. The girls had a host of friends that also made regular appearances. It was a wonderful time. An endless party.

Everyone in the house had a record collection and we took turns playing our favorite artists. I first heard John Prine at one of these sessions. Wow!, he could tell a story, no matter how tragic, and still inject just the right measure of humor! He could make you laugh and cry, all in the same song. There was an endless list of other gems, like Ray Materick and Scott Merritt, both Brantford area natives, but no one affected me more than Prine. At the same time, this California Cowboy thing was happening and I embraced it whole heartedly. The Burrito Brothers, Poco, The Eagles, Dan Hicks, Commander Cody, and the New Riders of The Purple Sage received many hours of airplay in my living room. Asleep At The Wheel got me hooked on Western Swing. The elements of traditional country harmonies, mixed with a Rock 'n' Roll attitude felt quite natural to me. The direction of my writing started to take shape. I had many stories to tell. I simply had to listen and learn as much as I could. My first efforts were naive, but believable.

...Sometimes, the singer is green and lacking grace,
The youthful innocence slaps you in the face,
The song is just as real as your twenty years of pain,
It's like some magic potion,
Turned the time back in your brain...

WESTSIDE
2009 -FROM THE ALBUM -LOVE IS A DOG

I discovered, early on that writing in the third person, like Prine does a lot, gives you license to say just about anything you want to without having to admit ownership. It granted me access to a much broader palette. This was one of the first and most important lessons I discovered about song writing. I still didn't have a band but I was building a network of musical connections and a body of work. I played house parties every chance I got and of course there was always an audience at the party house.

Achieving your musical aspirations are 'a long time coming' when you live in a place where there is a limited creative scene. Geography dictates your exposure to other like minded participants. You have to have wheels to expand your knowledge. You have to have a job to pay for the wheels. The small town inertia is always there ready to devour your dreams.

There are dozens of great musicians here and in the smaller towns that surround the north shore of Lake Erie. Seemingly content, they are unknowingly stuck in a vacuum of their own making.

THE SLIDE

Finally, Massey Ferguson opened its doors and hired me. I was told that I had it made. The thing about working in a factory is it isn't really that hard. The majority of the tasks don't require a lot of skill, especially if its assembly work. The job only requires eight short hours a day compared the grueling twelve to fourteen hour days you often had to put in on the farm. I tried my hand at spray painting, press work and eventually settled on setting up the big machines for production. I have to credit Mr. Fowler from my first job in Burford for teaching me the working basics of a machine shop. It didn't matter to me that my job wasn't very intellectually challenging. The pay and the benefits were the best in town. It allowed me the time to hone my musical skills and bring home a big paycheck. A lot of songs were written to the rhythm of a punch press or the monotonous repetition of the assembly line.

Music On, World Off.

...Factory life, Punch in,
And buy yourself an automobile,
Factory life, punch out,
And try to tell the world how you feel,
You got a daytime job and bills to pay,
You got a loan on time and pills to stay awake...

FACTORY LIFE
1982 -FROM THE ALBUM -SUB LEVEL AUDIO BULK

Part of my 'growing up' plan was to settle in and make a meaningful commitment. Foolishly, I thought this would make my parents happy and proud of me. This has always been very important to me. Regardless of my road education I was still and always will be my Mom's little boy. I just wanted to prove to them that I could do something good. Obviously I had developed a need for acceptance and once again, forgot who I was.

It was in this confused state that I decided to get married and settle down. Lesley appeared to be the answer. She wasn't like the other girls I had been

167

with and my nineteen year old brain was convinced that she was what I had been waiting for.

The Boy has visited home to introduce the girl he intends to marry. She appears somewhat needy and not cut from the same cloth emotionally or intellectually as her partner.

Old Peter and Rita seem to be cautious about her as well. Even the Boy cannot help but sense something is off, but he is blinded by his unwavering determination to do good in the eyes of his parents and make up for his long absence.

What I sense, although seemingly sincere, is not the same pleasant emotion that the first girl had projected...

I married Lesley, one of the the girls from downstairs that year, in afterthought for all the wrong reasons. She was a bit shorter than me, with short blond hair and a massive smile. I guess we looked good together. Suddenly I had a 'set for life' job, a young wife and a nice pickup truck. Chevy pickup's are considered the vehicle of choice, where I come from. There was a lot of catching up to do and I had managed to do most of it in record time. I was locked in. What I didn't realize was that I was on my way to becoming one of 'them'. I didn't know much about my new wife either. How could I? It hadn't been a year from when we first met. I've always been the one to blindly jump in feet first and fine tune things as the need dictates. I still am that guy, but hopefully with a bit more wisdom. A month into the marriage I started to question my choice, but stubborn pride made me reluctant to admit my mistake so soon into the game. My flawlessly patient Mother would sympathize with me when I finally confessed my conundrum and say things like "don't worry, people change." I know for a fact that this is just wishful thinking. People don't change. At least not into what you want them to. It's not fair for you to expect them to. My decision to hang in there and ride it out proved to be quite a solitary task. Although there were many happy times, thanks to my mothers gift of patience I more than often gave in when things went south, just to keep the peace. I pretended to my friends and family that everything was just peachy. I didn't know shit. Much later in life I realized that living the truth is a whole lot easier than living the lie.

One evening there was knock at the door. Lesley answered it. There was a short muffled conversation,

"You better come and see this." she said.

My God!, it was Betty Ann from Trail! She had given birth to a little girl and wanted me to meet her.

That said, a two and a half year old little 'mini- me' poked her head into the doorway. There was no mistaking who the father was. This little dark haired, brown eyed doll was definitely mine. I was floored, though not nearly as much as my new wife.

Betty Anne assured me that she wasn't looking for money or support payments as it would mess up her application for government housing and single mother benefits. She had been raised in that environment. Her mother had chosen the same path much earlier. Later on, so would my daughter. Betty Anne truly believed it was the best thing to do.

In spite of government incentives and free public education, the cycle continues. I was in no position to argue the point and was given an open invitation to visit as much as possible to get to know my little girl, Shelby. Betty Anne remained a great friend for the time she had left on this planet. She married a nice guy and actually got out of the system. I was proud of her and visited them as much as I could.

BACK TO BURFORD

We had recently moved out of the party house into the village of Burford where I went to high school. One day I ran into a old school buddy at the corner store.

Stan Baka was a few years older than me. He was the coolest guy in town. Stan was tall and slim with long wavy black hair reaching down his back and wore small wire rimmed glasses. There was a slight gap between his two front teeth when he smiled. Mom said he looked like Jesus, which I took as a sign of approval. Although he never got the knack for walking on water, he was also a great guitar player. We talked about putting a group together along with his pal, Kevin Cosman. They had just parted ways with John Mars. Their former band was called 'John Mars And The Martians'. I saw them play at a high school dance and they were way out there. I was intrigued.

John Mars surfaced many years later and we have become close friends. He's an interesting guy, a non-objective painter, who loves to study music history, and the stock market. He adds to his many talents, proof reading. As I write, he is diligently going over my manuscript, madly eliminating commas, parenthesis and spelling errors. I have looked through his collection of already published biographies by actual famous people and found neatly penciled corrections in most of them.

Stan and "the Cos" shared a twisted sense of humor and had diverse musical influences from Zappa and Beefheart to Leadbelly and Howlin' Wolf. We practiced upstairs in the sewing room at Stan's place. He had recently gotten married and had a new child. We played acoustically, crowded around a 4 track reel to reel and started working out some Pure Prairie League, early Lynyrd Skynyrd stuff, a few John Prine songs and some obscure Lead Belly tunes. Gradually we started working on some of my tunes. It was great! Everybody sang. Two acoustic guitars, a bass and three part harmony. I was encouraged to write more and began introducing a new song or two, every week. After a long winter of rehearsals we were ready for the public. That early spring we did a show at the old party house in Brantford and it went over great! As it turned out, it would be our only show.

He is closer now, but still outside of my range. He visits his old home regularly and I immediately sense a new awakening in him. His creativity has reclaimed it's rightful position. The music has taken control and he willingly allows it to fill his dreams with light and color and a noticeable contentment. He pushes his other domestic concerns to a place I have no desire to access. I am only interested in the dream. For the first time, I wonder if I may somehow be allowed to influence the Boy or at least nudge him onto the right path...

In the long summer months it was customary to go down to Whitemans Creek, outside of Burford on Sunday afternoons to chill out with friends and party. It was a beautiful sunny day. I had my guitar and was lazily plunking out a few tunes in the cool shade down by the shallow, fast moving trout stream. A group of high school acquaintances that I had not seen since my school days were solemnly walking through the park. I was happy to see their faces after my long absence and happily greeted them. That's when I was told Stan had been killed earlier that day in a motorcycle accident.

There is a fragile thread that ties us to this mortal plain. For the first time, I became aware of it. This was the first step I truly took towards the concept of maturity.

The funeral was surreal. I remember riding to the grave yard with a group of friends softly singing old John Prine songs. "*...please don't bury me, down in the cold, cold ground..."* The music connected us but did nothing to comfort the collective realization that we were not after all meant to live forever. It was as if fate had pulled the carpet out from under me. Death did not apply to our kind. We were invincible. But none the less, the darkness had found one of my brothers. A great friendship and musical chemistry was disrupted. What a shame it had to end.

I long to comfort him in his despair and introduce him to my existence. Although my awareness lacks physical substance, it is as real as the light and sound in his dreams. I share the same emotions, happiness, joy, pain and loss. Perhaps, if I could reach beyond the curtain that separates us he will one day understand that death is not as finite as he is led to believe...

ANDY & MARLEY

Andy Jeans is a Burford boy. Implanted from Toronto, his folks were the only grown up hippies in town, right down to the VW micro bus with flowers and peace signs painted on it. His dad was a drummer and his mom, a supply teacher. She reminded me of Silvia Tyson (of Ian and Sylvia fame) with her long raven hair. Andy, on the other hand was blond and a little small for his age.

I was a few years older than Andy but we became close friends instantly. He had great taste in music and we shared the same bizarre sense of humor. Monty Python, SCTV, National Lampoon and bad Sci-Fi provided us with sufficient fuel to keep each other in stitches indefinitely. The absence of humor would make life unbearable. We injected it everywhere, like butter on bread.

One year I grew a bunch of pot in the neighbors corn field and Andy sold it for me. He pumped gas at The Hitching Post, a local restaurant, convenience store and gas station on the edge of town. From his little hut by the pumps you could fill up on gas, get your oil topped off and bring home a bag of dope without leaving the comfort and safety of your car. Andy had unintentionally invented the prototype for the first 'drive through'.

One hot July day, I went on an unexpected adventure with him.

The 401 Highway is the major artery that stretches from Windsor, through Toronto, then to Montreal and beyond. A group of friends and I were headed for the big 'T Nothin' to the legendary Maple Leaf Gardens. We had tickets for Bob Marley.

I was introduced to the music of Bob Marley by a Jamaican guy I had befriended. The local tobacco farmers had started bringing foreign help to work in the harvest through some kind of deal with the Canadian government. The new crop of pampered local kids thought it was beneath their station to work in the fields. Carlton Campbell III was cousins with Peter Tosh, who was an original member of

Bob Marley's Wailers. He was a Rastafarian and I grew to understand his Jamaican patois well enough to become his translator at most of the gatherings I would invite him to. Carlton turned me on to reggae music years before Eric Clapton introduced the world to 'I Shot the Sherriff' (a Marley song). In the wintertime, Carlton was part of the Wailers' road crew and later Peter Tosh's.

Just west of Toronto the traffic starts to get congested. We were just crawling along when I observed, two lanes over, a car pulled off to the side with the hood up. I realized it was my friend Andy just as the traffic started to roll past. I felt awful having to leave him behind but we were in the center lane and there was nowhere to pull over. We may have gotten an eighth of a mile further up when the traffic halted altogether. This was my chance. I jumped out of the car and ran back towards Andy and his disabled Chevrolet. He was staring into the engine compartment with his hands on his head when I tapped him on the shoulder. He almost jumped out of his shoes, but looked relieved when he saw it was me.

"C'mon! Leave the car here! Follow me!", I shouted over the traffic.

Without hesitation he abandoned his car and we started running through the stopped traffic to get to our ride. He had tickets to the same concert. Our ride was about twenty steps away when the cars started moving again. Undaunted, we got the bright idea to hitch a ride on the back bumper of a transport flat bed trailer so we wouldn't lose ground. The surrounding traffic and the truck picked up speed. It was going too fast to jump off. Andy looked over at me and shrugged his shoulders, "I guess we might as well enjoy the ride!" he shouted over the traffic. Much to the delight of my crew in the other lane we waved like the queen as we pulled ahead of them. Our driver had enough sense to pull in behind the truck and follow. Andy and I did our best Olympic gymnast impressions to entertain the audience behind us until the traffic finally slowed once more to a stop. That was our cue to jump off the truck and into the back seat of the waiting car. We got to The Gardens just in time and safely to our seats just as Marley and the I-Threes launched into the first song.

That, my friends is how you go to a Bob Marley Concert!

CH-CH-CH-CHANGES

Lesley and I had two sons over the next few years. I was five years into a marriage with two great kids and I was still miserable. I loved my children as much as any parent but I had grown up in a different direction from my wife, Lesley. I say 'different direction', but truthfully, we were from two different worlds. I guess I should have checked her inter-planetary passport before we got hitched. It wasn't her fault, after all, incompatibility is not a crime. I knew then I should take my lumps and get out, but once again I didn't. I could accept the option of living without her, but simply could not leave my kids.

Instead, I put together a great band with my old drummer friend, Ray Ovington and toured as often as I could. The road cures everything. KAOS was a heavy rock band. We played Zeppelin, Bad Company, Black Sabbath, AC DC and what practically every other band was playing on the circuit at the time. Some better than others. Lesley and I had moved to Harley, just 3 miles up the road from my parents house. Our place had a heated garage, a perfect spot for band practice.

My folks place provided a great escape for the kids and me when things at home got intolerable. Life was always normal in Mom's kitchen. My little brother and sisters entertained the boys and I would get a chance to garner whatever wisdom my parents could offer. We visited often.

THE TWISTER

On August 7th, 1979, the bands regular practice day was disrupted by a violent storm. It took out our power and telephone lines and devastated the landscape...

From my vantage point, high up in the old maple, I witness the destruction of the approaching tempest. It comes from the north west and rolls in like a tidal wave, tossing debris and destroying everything in it's path.

As the fury increases Rita herds the children into the tiny basement under the recent addition. Old Peter refuses to leave the kitchen. "If this house goes down, I'm going with it!" he stubbornly shouts. Rita cannot convince him to do otherwise and finally retreats into the basement to comfort the frightened children.

When the neighbors cattle barn is reduced to splinters My reflex is to brace myself against the relentless torrent. The old tree catches the wind like a huge sail, groaning and twisting. Some of the tree's younger brothers and sisters lose their grip and topple into each other. I became fearful of losing my beloved vessel and my old home. Two large pine trees are tossed like twigs towards the back of the school. I brace for impact. The old maple stands in defiance and absorbs the flying missiles like a valiant general defending the line. The tree shakes and rattles, but holds fast.

The storm passes over as quickly as it had come and the peaceful quiet and blue sky reclaim their rightful place. The school still stands, surrounded by a mountain of tree branches and twisted steel siding from the barn that was previously next door. Old Peter has been tossed across the kitchen like an unwanted toy. He slowly grunts and gets to his feet, shaken, but relatively unhurt. Rita tends to his bumps and scratches after leading the disoriented children back to the main floor...

Early next morning there was still no power or
phone. On my truck radio it was reported that a
tornado had ripped through parts of nearby
Woodstock and then moved south through Oxford
Centre, New Durham and Vanessa. My family home
was a mile east of New Durham, right on the outer
edge of its path.

I jumped in my truck and headed towards the old
homestead. Within a mile of the house the road
became impassable. The giant Maple canopy that
once shaded the road had entirely swallowed the
path. A mountain of gnarled wood and bright green
leaves blocked the horizon. I abandoned the truck in
the middle of the roadway and frantically began
climbing and crawling up, over and around the
devastation. Everything was out of place. The usual
landmarks were missing, houses, barns, concrete
silos, the United Church on the hill. All gone. I
surfaced in the tiny graveyard behind the house.
Two large horizontal pine trees had slammed into
the ancient maples in the back yard. At least some of
them they were still standing, although twisted and
visibly scarred. I distinctly remember saying a silent
thank you to them as I made my way pass. The
entire space beyond was green on green over a calm
clear blue sky. Climbing through the infinite rubble,
I finally found my way to the house. The main
structure was intact, although windowless. The front
door stood open. I swallowed hard, held my breath

183

and walked in. Dad was in his usual spot, leaning on the kitchen island with a bottle of port and a half full glass, smoking a cigarette. He was reading the paperback novel, 'Little Big Man', seemingly oblivious to the chaos around him. Mom and the kids were cleaning up the mess and surveying the damage. I let out my breath. The kids told wide eyed stories of flying cows and cars and what sounded like a roaring train passing over the house. They had watched in amazement from the single basement window that faced south.

It would be seven long weeks before power was restored. The twister had taken out a dozen of the huge steel Hydro towers that provided electricity to the area. The road was barricaded at our corner to keep out the curious. The next door neighbors house had also been spared, but his big cattle barn was gone as was everything else for a mile west to the village of New Durham.

With no electricity for weeks, crews of 'horse and buggy' Mennonites began the task of rebuilding. The air was filled with the sound of hammer and saw. A chorus of chainsaws replaced the silent void where the crickets, frogs and cicadas had filled the air. The twister had sucked the water out of the creek and deposited it's inhabitants elsewhere.

As part of our promo kit for the band, I used a quote

from the Brantford Expositor.

'... a storm ripped through our county yesterday and
left a path of destruction.
They said it was chaos...'
we're sorry...
KAOS

HARSH REALITIES

The next 3 years became a blur. Members of the band came and went. Six nights here, travel Sunday, six more nights there, travel Sunday and so on and so on, but we were making as much money as the guys back home in the factory. I wired home my pay weekly. We would be gone for 6 to 8 weeks at a time, usually in Northern Ontario or Quebec. The rest of the time would be a series of local gigs and then back to the North. That's rock n' roll.

The "Rock Star" trip was mental salvation from my turbulent home life, but trying to keep a band and your life together can be almost impossible at times. Egos and personal differences in the band created more drama than the joy of playing music alone could sustain. It seemed whenever we were on the brink of making it to the next plateau, someone in the band would decide to quit. I can't really blame anyone in particular. We had been on the same soul grinding northern circuit for over 3 years. We needed a change. This was going nowhere fast.

Before MTV, a Toronto television station launched a new weekly TV show called 'The New Music.' Every week J.D. Roberts and Jeanne Beker interviewed mostly T.O. bands or bands playing T.O. as well as new international acts visiting the area. We were seeing bands on the show that we had toured with. Some of them were opening shows for us. It was frustrating. It seemed like Toronto and the Queen Street scene was the place you had to be if you were going to get picked up by a record company. We were the road veterans, but totally off of the radar.

Our booking agent had us working 'B' rooms on the the Northern Circuit and we could see no foreseeable advancement. Reality was, he didn't really have any 'A' rooms to book us into. After all, he ran the agency from the back room of a hot dog joint. That should have been our first clue. We wisely cut ties with him and decided to try it on our own until we could find a suitable agent to represent us. Our great track record made it was surprisingly easy to fill in the calendar, all the while managing to stay closer to home and Queen Street. I balanced the slow times with my job at Massey Ferguson.

How did I manage to tour for three years and keep my job, you may ask? Mainly, shift work and benzedrine to make up for the lost sleep, but in reality the 'set for life' job was a bust. There wasn't much of a job left to come back to. Whenever I did return, we were either laid off or on strike and eventually the plant closed altogether. The town was thrown into an economical depression. The unemployment rate was the highest in the country. This put an even greater strain on my home life. If absence makes the heart grow fonder it did not apply to my relationship. The distance between Lesley and me grew further every day. In desperation I started a renovation business to generate extra income in the down time, roofing and siding mostly. It provided a regular paycheck and flexible hours. After three years under the stage lights, there is nothing more humbling than roofing in a snowmobile suit in November.

The band became more selective about taking engagements. We concentrated on the jobs that would take us to the next level. As our regular gigs wound down, the renovation business became my main source of income for the next few years. In the summer months it is rewarding work. There is something gratifying about building and repairing things with your hands. Dealing with things you can see and touch, but the music never stopped running through my head, like electricity humming through a wire, only slightly disappearing into the background but always present.

There is a continuous sound track behind everything I do. I walk and breath, hammer and saw in rhythm. My skills as a carpenter and woodworker have kept the wolves from the door on many occasions. I am fortunate to have these skills to fall back on, unlike some of my other musician friends. As they say in the entertainment business, 'Don't quit your day job.'

THE SHIFT

In 1982, thanks to my beloved Pierre ET who started this whole journey, a new Canadian Constitution and Charter of Rights was introduced. Wonderful news for almost everybody except for one little loop hole which, between the lines loosely stated; "you cannot be refused a job because you are not affiliated with a union" Sounded liberating at the time to us musicians. We tore up our American Federation of Musicians union cards. No more contracts. No more union dues. I don't think anyone, including the government could have anticipated what happened next.

Almost overnight the bars and clubs also broke ties with the union and voilà, we went from playing 6 nights a week to just weekends. A lot of the clubs started hiring strippers during the day to grace our former 'union only' stages. Some quickly realized it was just as easy and profitable to run strippers in the evenings instead of employing bands. Other clubs filled their slow evenings with karaoke, amateur nights, wet t-shirt nights and 'battle of the bands' competitions. This provided a respectful draw for the bar owners at a fraction of the cost. An 'exposure gig' for our band to showcase in Toronto became pretty much ' pay to play.'

Musicians are a fickle bunch and for the most part, not very good business men. Established bands were soon playing for half of what they used to demand just to keep working. With no union cards required, weekend bands popped up that would play for next to nothing, or just for beer. The bars could name their price. There was no such thing as paying union scale anymore. This drove the price for an established professional band even lower. What a shit show. The roots of our musical infrastructure were gone forever. Eventually even the radio stations joined in and Canadian Content was narrowed down to the handful of already established acts that had made onto the 'American Billboard Charts.'

Today there is no longer a roots based circuit out there to support a new band's desire to play full time and develop their skills. The veteran players that stuck it out have to play gigs with a different band every night just to survive, picking at the scraps of a once thriving profession.

The fallout is still evident over 30 years later. Clubs that once hosted polished, professional bands with a light show and a monster P.A. now provide small inadequate in-house sound systems, and most times nothing you would call stage lighting. A good number of the bands barely have enough experience or talent to hold a crowd. At best they provide background noise for the people texting in the front row. The clubs are getting smaller crowds, so they up their prices. The audience knows they are not getting quality entertainment for their eight dollar draft beer. God forbid, they should have to pay a $5 cover to see a better band. Shheeesh.

...You give away your privacy, and pay a monthly fee,
You rip the song right from my chest,
And hand it out for free,
One day you'll wake up in your bed and realize
There's nothing new out there,
and no one cares to try...

SPEED AND GASOLINE
2007 -FROM THE ALBUM -REDNECK LULLABY

THE NEW WAVE

Right when I thought the whole music scene had gone for a complete crap, a new group of musicians rose from the ashes like an angry phoenix and made a stand. No money? Who gives a fuck! No fame? Fuck fame! If you don't like us, Fuck off! The Punk Movement had arrived.

I was too 'over the hill' at 26 to fall in line but still young enough to get it. I admired their revolt. When most of us sheep just accepted what was being jammed down our throats, this bunch of rebels recognized that the corporations were taking away what had once belonged to all of us. The concept of Rock 'n' Roll. The rock legends we grew up with had become rich, old and fat parodies of themselves. My g-g-generation was now represented by some middle-age dude with a Rolex and a BMW.

Rock 'n' Roll was supposed to be fought in the trenches. Rock 'n' Roll was screwing in the back seat of your car. Rock 'n' Roll was playing slightly out of tune just enough to piss off your parents. Rock 'n' Roll was the voice of youth. This new raw sound embraced that conviction better than the 'Stadium Rock, Supergroup Crap' that was on the radio. Jeezzus!, some of that stuff was horrible, pretentious bullshit! It didn't reflect what was really going on in our dirty little world and I was overjoyed that at least some people hadn't fallen for it.

My landlady at the time was an old hippie from England. She rented us this small house in Harley that she had aptly named Maple Tree Cottage. How very British. I can't remember how I first met Neville, but I visited her often and we became very close friends. She always wore flowered gowns and glided, rather than walked across the room. I would often get into long intense conversations with her, lost in her mesmerizing accent. Her son John grew up in Britain in the middle of the Punk and New Wave movement which was just catching hold in my little pocket of North America. He was 19, and in his British punk paraphernalia was truly out of place in the small village of Burford where he attended High School. I know how that feels. Burford was always more than four or five years behind what was going on in the rest of the world. His record collection was full of albums he had collected there and brought with him from England. I was drawn to the songwriters like Elvis Costello, Ian Dury and Graham Parker. The Clash was awesome. The New York scene was exploding with groups like Blondie, The Ramones and Lou Reed. Talking Heads '77 blew my mind. It had been out for while, but off of my radar until young John introduced me to it. The sound was raw and honest, the lyrics, direct and to the point. There were bands up the road in Hamilton, like Teenage Head, The Forgotten Rebels, and Simply Saucer shaking it up. It was dangerous. It was raw. It was glorious.

I didn't relate to the look so much. I was a dad by then. I wasn't into the androgynous make up or the spandex look either. I was not from some industrial suburb or inner city. I wasn't from New York or London. I was just a long haired country kid from Southern Ontario.

One night I played the Talking Heads record for my drummer, Ray. We listened to it four times, over many beers and Ray turns to me and says, "I don't think the other guys in the band are gonna get it"

After a few more beers it was decided that we would have to pull the plug on KAOS. We started looking for some new guys. Time to put together a new band!

195

NEW DIRECTION

The new band took a while to pull together. We auditioned new musicians relentlessly. The polished experienced players were too old school for what we had in mind. We were looking for people with just the right amount of attitude. There was not a large pool of like minded musicians lurking about in Harley.

We invited a lead guitar player from Brantford to a 'try out'. We had heard of him through some mutual friends. He showed up with an old Fender Mustang and a distortion peddle. His playing was gritty and Keith Richards sloppy, but there was this distinctive, melodic quality hidden just under the surface. It was obvious he was being influenced by the same bands we were listening to.

Half way through the shakey audition Ray and I went outside to relieve ourselves. "What do you think, Ray?"

Ray took a sip of beer, looked over and laughed, "He's awful, let's keep him."

Tom Kerr was invited to join the band. I christened him the world's greatest bad guitar player.

The band rehearsed twice a week, Tuesday and Wednesday, so we could retain the new stuff we were creating. Ray lived at home on his parents' tobacco farm and we took over the 'strip room' for the winter. This was the heated room in the pack barn where they graded the cured tobacco into late autumn. I set up a reel to reel tape recorder so we could review the new material and pick out any weak spots. We went through a series of bass players until we settled on Mark Dekker. He used to play for another 'rival' band in Brantford. He had the right gear and an open mind.

Tom had a great ear for catchy hook lines and new guitar sounds and the show was slowly coming together. It kept my soul intact through the dark times. We were very fortunate to have a great rehearsal space. We could play as loud as we wanted out there on the farm. Another advantage was that we had our own sound gear. In those days bands provided their own sound and lighting. Ray and I had purchased the system from our previous touring band. The more sound and lights you had determined how much you should ask to be paid. It also made you look and sound far better than the less fortunate bands who had to rent theirs.

On the home front, I had taken advantage of a government retraining program developed for the thousands of out of work factory workers. I hung up my carpenters apron and went back to school. After a four hour adult equivalency exam I was awarded my grade 12 diploma. (I had left school mid way through grade 10.) I enrolled in a two year Print and Commercial Art course. I was going to College! I wondered about the validity of a high school education in that era, especially if you could condense four years of schooling into a four hour test.

College was a refreshing change from touring or factory work. Being a mature student also gave me license to call 'bullshit' when my instructor was shoveling it. I was relentless. Most of the teachers had never been in the real world. They had sailed straight through high school into teacher's college and right back into class. The few that had been in the outside environment had failed to advance in their given trades and came back to teach. My sincerest apologies to the great teachers out there.

The courses seemed to be designed to create workers, not leaders or innovators. Bee hive mentality. Fine with me. I would get my diploma first and acquire my business training in the trenches. The short hours, 9am to 2pm, provided a lot of time to spend with my kids and a convenient window for putting together a new band.

The entire city was in a financial bind. Money problems had broken up many happy marriages during that time and the strain was taking its toll on our already rocky relationship. I retreated from my wife and our financial woes as often as possible. It seemed I was fighting a losing battle. Unfortunately, neither of us possessed the tools to even attempt to fix this kind of dysfunction.

The band finally settled on the name, 'Plastic Diet' out of frustration. One day, after weeks of unsuccessfully trying to come up with a catchy moniker, we sat around my kitchen table feeling defeated. My young son, Josh was on the floor chewing on a toy.

"Hey Paul, your kid just took a bite out of his toy!"

I looked over, unconcerned and said, "Yeah, he's on a plastic diet" Bingo!

A club, up the road in nearby Paris, Ontario, The

Paris Inn, supported original music and gave us a monthly gig. Just what we needed to gel together a solid show. There was another new original group playing there regularly, Tom Cochrane and Red Rider. The 'Diet' managed to pack the place consistently. We had developed a great following and I had all my new school friends to invite to the shows.

It wasn't as difficult to get people to show up for a night of music in that era. In 1983 it's just what everybody did. Before online dating, you took your chances and went to the bar every weekend to meet your potential mate, in the flesh. What a concept. Analog dating.

The bulk of the local club owners still insisted bands to play top 40 crap, not that there was any science to explain why. They just couldn't see the changes and were more concerned with selling beer. We got around this problem by having two set lists, the one in our 'promo kit', listing all the top 40 songs that most owners expected to see, and in our guitar cases, the real list, more than half original songs mixed with a good chunk of what ever the hell we wanted. No one ever called us on it.

There was one popular club in Brantford that we kept trying to get into but they wouldn't have us because we were local and they catered to the 'slicker' Toronto bands. The owner didn't feel a local group would have the draw to fill their room. Undaunted, we rented the local Union hall to throw our own show and gave an invite to the owner. It was sold out to capacity, about 450. His bar only held half of that. He showed up that night, curious to find out why his bar was suspiciously empty. He changed his mind about hiring us. For the next few years we were working steady weekends and making pretty good money. Almost as much as when we were doing six nighters.

Our first independent album was released on cassette. This was before CD's, and vinyl cost a fortune to manufacture. Plastic Diet -'Sub Level Audio Bulk' did not fly off the shelves but it established us as an original group with promise. It was a collection of songs I had written in the factory, heavily influenced by Talking Heads. The 'Records On Wheels' store in Brantford put our poster in the front window to promote us. Our loyal fans filled the rooms wherever we played. We had cemented a solid underground following. Everything was falling into place.

In the meantime, I had graduated from college and took a job running a small print shop in Hamilton. The music scene there was much like the Winnipeg scene that I had witnessed years earlier. There were tons of clubs and lots of really great bands. I just had

201

to get a slice of it.

Even though I now had a 'real' job, nothing had changed for the better at home. Getting hitched at nineteen was a dumb idea. The dumbest move I had ever made. My rock n' roll dreams had never fit into her plan and her aspirations to become a suburban house wife never fit into mine. I guess the only thing we really agreed on was that we were a just a couple dumb kids when we tied the knot. I finally got the guts to call it quits. This time I really did it, but of course there is always a price. After ten years in an unhappy marriage, I left with nothing more than my guitar, my clothes and the haunting realization that my decision would impact the lives of my children. I moved into a single room in Hamilton. I had no car. I had left everything behind for the wife and kids.

That same year, our bass player quit. Without wheels there was no way for me travel back and forth to break in a new guy and the band just imploded. Back to the drawing board. In this game of life, I was batting zero. Time to wipe off the chalkboard and start over. I was miserable.

Almost over night, I was alone in a new town with no family or friends, just my guitar and a box full of songs. This feeling was not alien to me. I had been here before, but in the past, it had been by choice. I was down, at the same time excited about a fresh beginning, free to take on whatever this big city had to offer. Maybe this time I would get it right.

...And you are the loneliest soul in this town,
You're not going anywhere, but down,
Angels don't come around,
Angels don't come around,
Angels don't come around here...

BLUE MARTINI
2004- FROM THE ALBUM -BLUE MARTINI

The Boy visits home. He is finally free from the burden of an empty relationship, but under the surface very troubled about his decision to leave the children. He knows his only other option would be to continue on the same unhappy, troubled path.

Presently, I fear he has put himself into a bad place. Perhaps a door in his mind has opened, that is dark and unforgiving.

He has inherited his Mother's unwavering patience and optimism and puts on a brave face for the family. However, the perceived failure, due mostly to his own poor judgment, still torments him. When I try to reach him I am met with a wall of uncertainty.

What he does not know is that this part of his journey will make him stronger. The storm will pass. The sun will shine. Like the old tree, he has the ability to bend and twist and although there will be scars, he will still stand tall...

BAYTIDES

Downstairs from my tiny room in Hamilton was Baytides Café, a small 30 seat wine and beer bar near downtown.

Doug, the owner, made the best burgers in town and provided an atmosphere that attracted artists, writers and local celebrities. He was also my landlord.

The Café was in a dark, intimate, almost secretive back room, hidden from the busy Main Street. It was a perfect setting for it's creative inhabitants. My print shop was conveniently located in the alley out the back door. Tabby's Convenience was next door. Their sign proudly announced, 'We Never Close'. I spent many sleepless hours in the

J.P. Riemens

small arcade, hidden in the concealed cove behind the counter, playing 'Space Invaders' with the local hookers who would hang out there on slow nights after 3 in the morning. It was a treat having someone to talk to who wasn't trying to be someone else.

One evening in a conversation with Doug, I was telling him about 'The Ting' and 'The Banyan Tree' in Winnipeg, two similar size coffee houses that always had a singer/songwriter performing. I suggested that it would be a great fit for the café.

"Sounds like a great idea" he said, "You run it and I'll take care of the bar"

The deal was done. Doug let me install a small sound board, hang a couple speakers and set up a few microphones in the tight, lighted corner by the bar. Soon I was hosting a singer/songwriter night in the little room and it turned into a regular thing, six nights a week. It paid my rent. In addition to the great songwriters it attracted, the space was always bursting with other creative talent. Writers, actors, local TV personalities, painters, entrepreneurs, all crammed in shoulder to shoulder. It was our very own 'Little Bohemia'.

Female companionship was plentiful and for a while I took full advantage. This was 1984, just before the AIDS epidemic took hold and sex was still fun. It

206

was never a problem to find willing participants.

The responsibility of running the print shop coupled with my need to establish a new social identity proved to be exhausting. I would entertain the patrons until 1 or 2am every evening, then be up at 7am to open the print shop for 8am. I turned to amphetamines, a solution that I had employed while working shifts in the factory. I knew this was not a good idea, but my inner voice soon faded and I lost control. I fell into a pattern.

I started every day with 2 pills and a glass of water. At 5pm, I would close up shop and return to my room for a 2 hour nap, then 2 more pills, a shower and back to the Café for the evening. 'Show time!' I thought I was functioning quite well but eventually the drugs took their inevitable toll. My sleep diminished even further and soon I was eating the pills like candy. I ended up in the emergency room of Saint Joseph's Hospital one early morning after Doug had found me convulsing on the floor of my room. I can remember laying on the gurney in the hall, feeling ashamed and totally defeated. I made a promise that this was not how I was going to live the rest of my life. I wasn't finished yet. This was not how I wanted to be remembered. The next day, I quit.

I stumbled around for at least a month, without

missing a day of work. I would come home and spend a few hours in the café before bed. Aside from the occasional late night, I stayed clean and healthy. My strength and determination eventually returned and so did my songwriting. I bought an old VW Bug and started reconnecting with my old friends back home. My children were with me every other weekend and I visited my folks often. My inner voice grew stronger with every visit. I was back.

The Boy is home from the city for the weekend. He appears drawn and hollow as if recovering from a sickness. He is calm and determined in his dreams.

This evening, as he sleeps, I creep into his thoughts and try to initiate the beginning of a story for him to latch onto as his own.

In it he is sitting under the giant maple tree with his guitar, writing a beautiful song about love and friendship. I pray this image will assist in returning him to his chosen path. He smiles in his sleep and I believe in some small way, I have succeeded...

Grant Avenue Studio stood around the corner from the café and the folks working there would occasionally come over for food and a glass of wine. At the time Daniel Lanois and his brother Bob owned the place. I had no idea who may have visited in those days, but I know now that Dan was working with Rick James, Brian Eno, U2 and David Byrne (from Talking Heads) to name just a few. All this fame, just a few short blocks away! I'm happy I wasn't aware of who may have been in the audience while I was stumbling through a new song. I would have been paralyzed.

Some of the Baytides alumni achieved great success and are still rockin', writing books, selling paintings or working in theater and film. My good friend Edgar Breau and his band Simply Saucer are touring North America as I write this in 2018. Surrounded by so much creative talent was the perfect atmosphere to hone my craft as a songwriter. I made it my goal to introduce a new song every night. Once again, I was the student, the small audience my gauge for success or failure.

PAMELA

I first met Pamela in '85 at Don Cherry's Grapevine on Main and Walnut where she was a waitress. The first time I saw her, I was blown away. Her long curly blond hair, athletic body and my God!, what a smile! She wasn't like any of the other city women I had met at Baytide's Café. For one, she was the same age as me. The younger girls I had been dating lacked her sophistication. She had the essence of a 50's or 60's screen star, wholesome, yet sexy as hell. It was so relaxing to have a conversation with someone from my own generation, someone that understood my deep country roots. She had grown up in the small farming town of Palmerston and had endured many of the same growing pains that came with moving into a big, lonely city. I felt peaceful when

I was with her and we became a steady couple within a month. I had found a true soul mate. Everybody at the café said it wouldn't last 6 months. I had endured many turbulent romances during my stay there and I don't believe anyone expected I was capable of being monogamous.

I moved in with Pam into her small loft apartment at the base of the Niagara Escarpment. We took day trips out to see my daughter, and had my sons, Josh and Isaac over every other weekend. Often we took the boys on outings to explore the waterfalls and dozens of trails that wind through the hills. Small adventures, we called them. Pam would pack food and drinks and with our trusty rope we would tackle the wilderness. It was the places we found off of the trails that were the most fun. The rope came in handy whenever we got into a spot where we had to climb up or down a rock face to find a secret cave. The kids loved it.

Everyone eventually comes to a point in life where they wonder what would have happened if they had made different choices. My relationship with the kids had never been better. What I regret the most is enduring the last 5 years of my failed marriage. I'll never get that time back. My decline into the 'dark place' had also taught me a valuable lesson. I made a sincere oath to myself not to waste another minute of my life trying to be someone else.

Pam has been my partner now for more than half my life. Everything material and emotionally satisfying in my life is the result of this mutual commitment. The blood, sweat and tears is mixed with a healthy balance of laughter. She tolerates my ups and downs and takes me as I am, as I do her, sharing both pain and pleasure without exception. When I'm away and I think of home, it's always her face I see first.

THE ART OF THE DEAL

One of my new acquaintances from Baytides, Ed Polonek, became my business mentor. He was an entrepreneur and specialized in corporate takeovers among other things financial.

The owners of the print shop that I was managing had informed me that it was to be closed for good in 3 months and I would be out of a job. I had absolutely no money saved up. Every penny I had was paying off things from the marriage I had left behind. Ed took it upon himself to become my guide. We would meet in the cafe as he walked me through a plan to achieve ownership of my own print shop.

J.P. Riemens

Step one: Negotiate a deal with the present owners and offer to buy the business name and client list for a dollar. They were closing anyway, he explained. I followed his instructions and to my surprise they agreed without hesitation. One dollar. Now I had clients, but no print shop.

Step two: Find a bankrupt print shop, which I surprisingly happened to discover almost immediately. I felt like someone was watching over me. Done.

Step three: Negotiate a buying price based on 10% of the value. I nervously submitted my meager bid to the creditor and won. Of course, I didn't have the money on hand. I had 24 hours to deliver.

Step four: Approach the owner of the building where the bankrupt business resided and offer to sell him your bid. It was a good deal. The owner would cover the cost and in return, lease the space and equipment back to me. Ed suggested they would be happy to invest in the equipment if it meant having a secure tenant. I set up a meeting with the landlord and just as Ed said, he went for the whole deal! Now I had a fully equipped shop, clients and absolutely no working capitol. "Not a problem" he told me.

Step five: "All you have to do now is apply for a government guaranteed small business loan."

I did, and within a week I had 5000 dollars to work with and no payments or interest for a year! I had only spent one dollar of my own money when I was handed the keys to my own business! Wow!

Pam quit her waitressing job to join me in the print shop. Ironically, the new shop was next door to Don Cherry's where we first met. Together we worked endless hours, trying to turn the small business into something that could support our dreams. Spending twenty four hours a day with each other only strengthened our relationship. It was uplifting having someone to lean on. "You and me against the world, baby."

Half of the fun of running a print shop is the characters that walk in off the street. One of my first customers was The Hamilton Jewish News. Coming from my sheltered life in Harley, I grew up actually believing that Jewish folks only lived in New York and were mostly comedians. Imagine my surprise. As an inquisitive new business owner, they were always ready to offer me helpful business advice.

Mr. Braille, who managed the newspaper, once told me, "You're not officially in business until you've had two bankruptcies and a fire." Oy!

One afternoon these two older bearded guys show up in full hippie regalia. They wanted a price on tiny labels that read, 'Property of The Church of The Universe'. Brother Micheal and Brother Walter ran the church. Micheal could recite the new Canadian Constitution inside and out and explained that pot smoking was one of their religious Sacraments, therefore any contraband distributed by the church to members of the congregation was legal in a court of law. Thus the need for the identifying labels. While he explained this, Brother Walter rolled a joint and lit up.

I nervously told them, "Hey guys, this is a business and I have other customers that could walk in at any time, so maybe that isn't such a good idea."

By the time Micheal finished debating why it was indeed a revolutionary idea, the joint was done. In a haze of smoke we agreed on a fixed price. I printed their labels for years.

A coincidence perhaps, but in 1801, before my arrival here, a man named Abraham Dayton applied for a land grant claiming to be a Quaker. He was awarded a large tract of land where the village of New Durham now stands. It was later revealed that Mr. Dayton was not a Quaker at all and had created his own cult like following, The Universal Friends...

I wrote music constantly, but soon decided to take a

break from playing shows. I had to concentrate on keeping this new business afloat. I was content for a while, but like any true musician there is always a burning need to entertain an audience. The music I write is meant to share, to raise a brow, to break a heart, to draw a smile. This addictive need never diminishes. I believe it must be part of my DNA, as natural to me as the need to breathe oxygen.

SHATTERED

The summer of 1989, my father took ill and his chances of recovery didn't look good. We were visiting him in the hospital in Brantford and I fully expected I would be saying my last goodbye.

The Spinks / Ali fight was on TV in the waiting room. Ali looked overweight, old and tired. He was trying to wear Spinks down, but Spinks had his youthful determination and a visible hunger for the title. It was both sad and painful to watch the legendary champion at the end of his career.

I was paged on the intercom in the waiting room to receive a phone call. My youngest son, Isaac had been in an accident and was being airlifted to McMaster Children Hospital. I vaguely remember a weight falling over me as if gravity had betrayed me and quadrupled. Time stopped for me that day. I have no recall of the trip from Brantford General Hospital to McMaster's in Hamilton. I barely remember the surgeon explaining my son's injuries. I was jolted back into reality when the blip, blip blip of the heart monitor changed to a solid tone.

My father and my son died within fifteen minutes of each other.

I drifted in and out of self awareness for what seems like an eternity. Losing a parent is inevitable, but there is no way to prepare yourself for something as devastating as losing a child. All the kind words and support held no comfort.

I share his grief as I am swept back to another dark time. It is 1820 and almost everyone in the village has taken ill. The nearest doctors and hospital are in the city of Brantford, a long days ride on the dirt road they call The Quaker Trail, through the village of Burford and over the Grand River by ferry.

The sick are instead, brought to the school and I am charged with becoming the resident nurse along with my helper, young Mary Force. The same Mary Force whose identity I had borrowed for my visit to the Boy.

Over an 18 month period I helplessly witness almost half of my cherished students and many younger children from the village perish, including seventeen year old Mary. The weight of the loss still reverberates in my soul. The contaminated bedding and clothing is set ablaze in the small field behind the school which would also become their final resting place. Years later, I chose it as mine.

Their young souls do not inhabit the old maple as mine does, perhaps because, unlike me, they had somewhere else to go...

I grew to become fearless of anyone or anything. Nothing could hurt me that could possibly be more painful than losing my child. I reasoned that the worst thing imaginable had already happened and that the rest of my life would be a breeze. This revelation, right or wrong, was what eventually brought me back into the land of the living. I also credit Pamela and The Niagara Escarpment for helping me on the return journey. Every evening we walked endlessly along the Bruce Trail across the street from our loft. Stone cliffs on one side and 'Old Hamilton' neighborhoods on the other. There wasn't much conversation, but the silent companionship was healing. Most evenings we would climb up the 256 steps at the end of Dundurn Street and view the city lights from above. One such night, back in our loft, I dusted off my guitar and started playing again. The soundtrack, although melancholic, had returned like a long lost friend's familiar voice.

Playing new music to a listening audience was also very healing. It thrilled me when anyone would request one of my original songs.

"Play that one again about the girl and her dog" someone would ask.

Sometimes I would have no idea what song they were talking about, and one night I realized that my style of writing left the door open for individual interpretation. The song they had asked for may have really about my friends Holley and Lucy, but the listener had applied the lyrics to suit their own vision.

I now do what I can to keep that door open. I have been inspired many times by a listeners interpretation. My audience is intelligent and creative and quite capable of creating their own story. All I provide is a four minute photo.

I feel strongly now, that my gift was enlightened by this hopeless tragedy and in some small way, I try to honor my precious lost ones whenever I put pen to paper.

THE SECRET

My father had a huge collection of stories that he loved to tell. His favorite ones would be repeated until I could recite them almost word for word. He had also grown to be wise and would answer my questions with certainty and without hesitation...

In the year 1927, prohibition in Ontario officially ended. Up until the early 70's, the provincial government in their wisdom had concluded that the common man should not be tempted by a cornucopia of displayed alcohol. It was all kept tucked away in the backroom warehouses. Out of sight, out of mind, I guess.

When you entered a Liquor Control Board of Ontario store back then, you would be greeted by a featureless, empty room except for the center island counters. Upon finding your poison of choice on the board that surrounded the upper half of each wall, your task was to write your order out on the small yellow piece of paper provided. Each brand had its own unique code. Upon completion, you would then bring your order to the main counter and an LCBO representative would go deep into the back room and present your order in a plain brown paper bag, away from the prying eyes of the next customer. It was a solemn task and conversation was discouraged.

Old Peter was a lover of Benson and Hedges Cigarettes and Brights, Grape and Cherry Port Wine. He had memorized the code number for the wine.

On his 80th birthday, I asked my father what the secret of his longevity was. Without hesitation, he told me,

> "Marry a young woman
> and never forget this number;
> 772-B."

INTO THE LIGHT

Having compiled a catalog of original songs large enough for an entire show, I decided to quit playing cover songs altogether. I became dedicated to recording as much as possible, to get the songs out there. It was more difficult to get gigs, but for a songwriter so much more rewarding. I had no desire to be like most of the other acts in town, endlessly playing bad Beatles covers and every popular party song ever written only to be compared to the original produced version. I always thought of it mostly as bad karaoke with a guitar. Not for me.

An acquaintance of mine, Mike Northcott, had heard my act one night and asked if I would come to his little basement studio and record some demos. In one evening we recorded rough versions of around 30 songs. Mike and I narrowed down the list and came up with a plan. We would put some players together, go to the country and track an album on the May24 weekend in my Mom's kitchen. Mom was away for the holidays and we could turn the whole place into a studio. Mike introduced me to Randy Hill, Laurel Arbuckle, Mark Foley and Jaimie Sulek, to make up the group. I invited my high school music class buddy, John Givens and presto, we had a band.

The result was 'Mom's Kitchen', a rootsy, fiddle and mandolin driven fun fest, with a good serving of bluegrass and traditional country. A far cry from the rock influenced 'Sub-Level' album, but it was honest, genuine and different than anything anyone else was doing. It felt so right playing music again in the old kitchen where I used to audition for my Mom. Everything sounded natural and authentic, right down to the rattle of the oven racks when the bass hit a low note.

The entire weekend was a big party. I had bought multiple cases of beer and had a bag of pot the size of my head, which I had grown out in the corn field the previous summer. Pam and her girlfriend cooked for us and we played endlessly.

The Boy has filled the old school with

225

musicians! The glorious sound vibrates
through the old wooden timbers and deep into
the roots underground. Joyous laughter fills
the air around me. An air of confidence has
replaced regret and dismay. His companion
Pamela shares the emotion.

There is much more than music happening
here. This is a celebration, a letting go of the
past and a welcoming of the present. A rebirth
of sorts...

At one point we took a break to watch 'Saturday Night Live', then played on until daylight. After a short nap and a country breakfast we dove right back in. Everyone involved was pumped. I wish it could have been filmed. It was magical.

Mike then invited me to help digitally edit and master the record. I was hooked on the process right away. It was so much like the computer programs I used in commercial art, except with sound instead of pictures and type. By the time we were done I was making suggestions that Mike had never thought of. This part of the recording process still brings me pleasure.

The resulting cassette, 'Mom's Kitchen' got passed around and ended up in the hands of Maureen Doidge. She and her husband Bob had taken over

Grant Avenue Studio from Dan and Bob Lanois.

Maureen invited me to come in and record a song for the upcoming 'Hamilton Music Scene' compilation CD. This was my second introduction to a professional studio. The first was years earlier when Tom Kerr and I recorded two songs for a 45 RPM vinyl single.

The historic studio was awesome and the session players were world class. I became obsessed with the recording process, which becomes another story, later on. This led to a string of singles, released on the Roto-Noto Records label as Ugly Bob's Little Big Band. None of the tunes are that memorable to me, but with every recording session I garnered a bit more knowledge of what was required to put together a great piece of music.

'Ugly Bobs Little Big Band' was the crossover group between 'The Honolulu Masters' and later 'The Bar Flies'. We played a lot of Western Swing. I had been a big fan of Asleep At The Wheel since their first record. The style sits somewhere in between Blues and Rockabilly. The tempo had to be precise, too slow it's Blues, too fast it's Rockabilly. It's a lot more difficult to find that pocket and stay there than you would imagine, but when the band hits the pocket, it is heavenly.

Randy Hill played mandolin, Laurel Arbuckle on upright bass and my buddy and old friend, Jace Ford on joined us on drums. Jace's former group, 'Black Creek' was one of my favorite 'Newgrass' bands in the 70's. They had played at my wedding reception which was arguably the happiest part of the entire marriage. We were a great acoustic, upbeat band with rootsy four part harmony. Once again we were the only group around doing this kind of stuff and it was all original.

Jace followed his wife to Vancouver Island a year later and yet another band folded just as we were picking up momentum. I must admit my inability to hold a band together may appear to be a fatal flaw. I take full responsibility. Even in a city as big as Hamilton there are not enough shows to give anyone financial reward equal to time invested. Anyone who believes they can convince a group of individuals to follow their own personal agenda without compensation requires a huge ego. Although I have a keen awareness of my self worth, my ego has never fully developed.

THE HARLEY HILTON

We eventually had saved enough money to purchase my childhood home in Harley from my Mom in 1991. Pam and I had been escaping the city on weekends and she really loved the place. My old friends Mike and Sandy had moved into his folks' homestead at the other end of the road. They had two sets of twins, two years apart. They also had one of those old monster big screen TVs with the huge satellite dish parked outside on the side lawn.

Mike's truck trailer business had done well and with Sandy there to iron out the bumps it continued to grow. It had come a long way from the first trailer we built in the old pack barn at his brothers farm. I remember spray painting it and how high everyone got in the unventilated barn.

On occasion, Pam and I would give our friends a well deserved break and babysit for them. The kids would squeal with delight at bedtime when I would tell them made up stories about uncle Bob's milk cows, Mooriel and Mooreen. After the kids were asleep, we would watch movies on the big screen, which was a real treat for us. We had tossed our old Granada rental TV to the curb five years earlier. It felt like I had come home, hanging out with my old friends then taking the short ride down the deserted gravel road to our bed. After 10 years in downtown Hamilton, we knew we were ready for the sticks.

I rejoice! The Boy has come home to stay. He brings with him his companion Pamela. It has been a long wait but I have always hoped that our connection, albeit passive would somehow draw him in. Pamela is indeed sensitive to the Boy's aspirations. She quietly overlooks his misgivings and fortifies him when he is weak. I wonder what she would think if she knew of my ethereal existence?

He possesses a new calmness about him where there used to be frustration. There is a great sense of pride in the Boy. He has achieved many of his goals on the strength of his convictions and without any outside financial help. Pamela continues to support and inspire.

The muse has been reawakened and he creates daily. I look forward to entering his dreams with regularity...

In 1801 my homestead had been a church and later a school. The existing structure was erected around 1807 after the first structure was destroyed in a fire. It had remained a school until 1965. My parents bought it in a silent auction in '66 for 1200 dollars.

The yard is a country acre, surrounded by ancient twisted maple trees, some almost as old as the original white building. One old tree is over 70 feet high and towers over the house. The trunk is fourteen feet in circumference. I call it Old Mother. It creates some of the air we breath. It's root system surely reaches into our water source just as it has also woven a path through the old graves out back and under our home to the front yard. Sometimes I talk to it like an old friend.

There is a single row of stone markers in the small graveyard bordering the back yard. The stones date back to the mid seventeen hundreds and early into the eighteen hundreds. They are mostly the children of United Empire Loyalists who settled here before and after the war of 1812. They were victims of a disease breakout, quarantined in the school and

231

J.P. Riemens

buried out back. One of the stones reads Elizabeth Watts, born 1767, died January 2, 1856. Exactly 100 years before the day I was born. Another stone has the name Mary Force. She was only seventeen and although I know it is impossible, I feel we have somehow met. For all the Bob Dylan fans out there, one stone belongs to Robert Zimmerman.

I feel as if my trespass into his dreams have indeed achieved impact. The stream of knowledge acquired on my little intrusions may indeed flow both ways. The Boy's interest in the history of the little school almost seems like he is trying to decipher my existence. Today, he pulled his automobile into the drive, climbed out with a knowing smile, looked up and whispered, "Hello Old Mother". Of course he speaks to the old maple, but I wonder. Is this just an appreciation of nature or is he indeed acknowledging a presence?..

WELCOME HOME

Even though Pam and I grew up in the country there were a lot of adjustments to consider. We had become used to the conveniences of big city life.

There is no pizza delivery out here. If you forget to bring home the milk or bread it's a ½ hour drive into town. If it's after 6pm you have to drive an hour round trip to Brantford or Woodstock. And then there's the critters...

We had settled in comfortably after our first year. Our two black labs, Tesla and Jet guarded the house with ferocity when we were away. Any intruders entering our driveway would be met by our fearsome protectors with their loud barking and menacing wagging tails. God save you if you traveled without dog treats.

Late one evening there was a ruckus. The 'girls' were very disturbed at whatever was outside and sounded the alarm. Pam rolled over in the cool comfort of the blankets and mumbled, "Paul, go see what's wrong with the dogs."

I jumped out of bed to investigate and try to settle them down, but they insisted there was danger on the other side of the door...

In my first years here at the school there are many perils. Wild bears and wolves roam the night, but the more common problem is the rattlesnake.

The local farmers have taken to releasing pigs into the wild. The pig's skin is impervious to snake bite and they seem to like the taste of snake.

As the snake population decreases, the problem now is the dozens of feral pigs that are destroying the carefully tended crops. The farmers have organized a hunt...

Fumbling through the closet, I pulled out the trusty Cooey 22 single shot rifle I had received as a present on my 12th birthday. I wasn't taking any chances. I slipped out the door, my back to the wall like the glorious bastard I was, pointing the gun, first to the left then the right as I had seen in so many combat movies.

Then "WHOOHEEEEEE!", the sound was off to my left towards the back yard, "WHOOHEEEEEE!"

I froze...

It sounded just like the Clovis Creature from those old badly animated Hercules cartoons that used to come on TV just before Hammy Hamster, not unlike the sound of an old farmer clearing his throat and preparing a good spit. Hercules was nowhere to be seen.

"WHOOHEEEEEE!". I broke out in a cold sweat.

Searching for the source of the sinister sound, I finally pinpointed the location as my eyes began to adjust to the darkness. It was in the huge maple tree that hung over the garage. High in the tree, a lone possum was attempting to rob eggs from a nest and the angry birds were dive bombing him. A dark silhouette against the blue/black sky. He was fighting them off, arms flailing, like King Kong with a long hairless tail, "WHOOHEEEEEE!"
Man! I was so relieved I just stood there for a while, frozen under the porch light chuckling nervously to

and at myself. I had almost regained my composure when I came to the realization that I was totally naked, outside, with a rifle, under the porch light, and I could hear a car coming up the gravel road! A neighbor, no doubt. I gracefully backed through the door and into the house, unloaded the rifle and put it away. There are some things you don't want to have to explain.

When I crawled back into the safety of my bed, Pam, murmured, " What was it honey?"

"Oh, it was just a damned old possum stealing bird eggs."

"Why didn't you shoot it?" she replied.

"It got what it came for and left", I muttered.

I did not mention the sinister Clovis Creature and went back to sleep.

I have not had the opportunity to see very many naked men in my 89 years on the surface. It appears my memory is still quite functional as I cannot seem to wash this vision from my mind. Being vulnerable in one sense and empowered with a rifle in another.

Other than the visual, I believe the Boy has

lived much of his life to date in this state.
Every time he introduces a composition to new
ears for the first time, it is his soul that is
bared, his guitar the weapon, his audience the
creature...

The 'Harley Hilton' became an escape for a lot of my
Hamilton friends. Pam and I welcomed guests every
weekend. The house was filled with music and
laughter again. Whenever visitors came for the first
time from the city, it was always the same thing. A
car would pull into the lane, we would hear the car
doors slam, the dogs would bark a few times, then
stop, (usually for a potential head scratch from
whoever just arrived). Then instead of a knock on
the door, nothing for a long period of time. When
my curiousity would lead me outside to investigate,
the newbie guests would be out there, standing in
the quiet absolute darkness, wowing at the stars
while the dogs sniffed at their feet. I confess, I am
still guilty of doing the same thing occasionally,
when I come home late from playing a show.

I built a rustic wrap around covered porch from
rough cut lumber I had helped cut at a local sawmill.
One day we christened the finished creation by
having a porch warming party. In preparation I was
cleaning up the last bits of scrap and cutoffs from
the lawn. Pete and Stella, my next door neighbors
since childhood, were baling hay in the field that

separates our property. Pete, now about 75, on the tractor, Stella was on the wagon. The tractor stopped. From my front lawn I could hear Stella shouting obscenities at Pete as she climbed off the wagon and stormed off towards their house, spouting another volley of curses that could make a sailor blush. Unaffected, Pete spotted me, grinned and waved me over. When I got up to him he motioned for me to jump on the wagon and started moving. I could see our guests starting to arrive and thought, "What the hell, it's a small field", and I took over the job of piling the hay bales. Pam was welcoming the arrivals and looking around for me until someone spotted me off in the field and pointed it out. I could only laugh at their confusion and kept piling. Years earlier, at the beginning of my story, I had earned the 15 dollars to buy my first guitar on this very wagon.

The porch soon became a regular meeting place on Sundays for songwriters from the surrounding area. Most Sundays there would be as many as a dozen songwriters and guests, passing the guitar around to play to their latest creation. Food on the barbecue. Beer in the cooler. Original, acoustic music, interrupted only by the occasional farm tractor or combine on its way to a neighboring field. Heavenly.

I had been concerned that moving out here would limit my exposure to other musicians but it was the exact opposite. Our very own music scene was developing. Music goes where the music is.

THE DRIVE

In 1985 the 403 highway was completed between Woodstock and Hamilton. My place is 7 minutes south of the main artery and it takes me around 50 minutes to get to downtown Hamilton from home.

When the road was built, it split a number of farms in half, leaving the house on one side of the 4 lane and a long drive to the nearest on/off ramp to get to the barn on other side. It created a wall of tar and tin between friends, fields and neighbors.

I made the trip to and from Hamilton daily for over 25 years. It was never a hectic drive. There wasn't much traffic between my place and the city back then. The real problem was if you needed to get from Hamilton to Toronto or vise versa. The

sanctity of my VW chariot has never been defiled by
the intrusion of a cell phone. If anyone needed me
they could leave a message at home or at the office.
Driving in between those two points was my
precious alone time, when I could daydream if I
wanted to or simply plan for what lay ahead.

When I was playing regular shows, my drive home
would be at 3am when the highway was totally
deserted. There is a huge stretch of road between
Copetown and Brantford without the convenience of
an off ramp. I call it 'No Man's Land'. Somewhere
near the middle is a small white house, so close to
the four lane that at night you can see what they are
watching on their big screen TV as you drive by. In
the daytime I would occasionally see the occupant at
his backyard barbecue, apparently no longer aware
of the thundering transport trucks and cars whistling
past, not 100 feet from his ass.

I can see your TV flicker blue
From the freeway,
Who on earth would think,
To build a road so close to you,
There are no exit signs,
No way for me to find,
Directions to this place,
And I've been lost for days...
People on this highway,

Just go one way or another,
Nobody wants to take the time,
To go anywhere in between,
But here in No Man's Land,
You're Barbequin',
And watering your lawn,
To the sound of the world movin' on...

NO MAN'S LAND
2007 -FROM THE ALBUM -REDNECK LULLABY

You have to wonder about those displaced souls who may have stared out into the quiescent wilderness years previous and concluded this would be the best place to build a home. For some, the roots had been planted too deep to move away.

My drive home has been carefully measured and requires two tall boys of beer to complete. For the late nights I would buy them in advance and carefully place them in the drivers side door pocket to be opened only after I passed the last junction leaving Hamilton. I no longer practice this, but still refer to the trip as a two beer drive. The phrase is now reserved strictly as a unit of time measurement. On occasion I listen to the radio but usually I preferred silence and sometimes I write songs in my head.

One snowy night I was doing just that. The lyrics coming to me as if I was attached to some cosmic

241

transmission tower. The lyrics were so odd I knew if I didn't write them down immediately they would be lost forever. My second tall boy signaled that I was approaching the off ramp at Brant Road 25. As soon as I hit the ramp I pulled over into the snow, put my beer in the door pocket and frantically searched for something to write on. A pencil was located in the dash but the only paper I could find was Canadian Tire money, a whopping 10 cent bill. Determined not to lose the lyrics I frantically started scratching them onto the orange bill, line after line. It was a nonsensical tune but none the less, I kept writing.

"Knock Knock", someone was wrapping on my window! I looked out to see an OPP officer, shivering in the cold.

"Is everything all right sir?" (Wow. They call me Sir, now)

I rolled down the window and said, "Yes officer, the only thing wrong is that I'm getting old and if I don't write this down I'll forget it by the time I get home."

I then explained that this was my cut off and I was seven minutes from my driveway.

"OK, just making sure you weren't stranded out here", he replied.

As I drove away and reached for my beer I had to wonder what he would have thought if he had read my notes...

> ...I know you don't want me,
> So why don't you leave me,
> I'm just a big stick in your spokes,
> Your mom and your dad,
> Think I'm evil and bad,
> Your friends think I'm some kind of joke
> I'm an internet virus,
> I'm Billy Ray Cyrus,
> I just don't know when to go home,
> I'm a free liquor shot,
> I'm the luck you ain't got,
> If Love is a Dog, You're The Bone...

LOVE IS A DOG
2009 -FROM THE ALBUM -LOVE IS A DOG

From my vantage point in the highest branches of the tree, I hear the faint rumble and hum from the highway to the north. Occasionally, I may also hear a train off in the distance, even though I have discovered it is at least 10 miles away.

Many evenings, on cool summer nights, the Boy joins me on the front porch when he

243

J.P. Riemens

returns from the city, to soak in the silence and witness the stars. During those peaceful witching hours the quiet is absolute and as comforting as a soothing elixir...

SUZY

I was at a get together on the 8th Concession. Tony and Margret Fowley had little parties quite often. They loved music. Originally from County Cork in Ireland, their names pronounced in their accent would be more like TowNee and Maagrit. We always partied outside around a bonfire because Maagrit had laid the law down to TowNee, "I won't have ye hoodlums fekkin' up me furniture."

I was sitting around the campfire singing a few songs when a stranger sat down and introduced himself. Darrell really liked my stuff and I ended up giving him a copy of my tape, 'Mom's Kitchen'.

The next day this new acquaintance pulled into my drive and like an old friend handed me 12 beers. A girl got out of the other side of the car.

"This girl needs to meet you, So here you go, Buddy. I'll be back later", and Darrell took off down the road leaving the beer and the girl standing in the lane. Wow! Now that's a friend!

That was how I was introduced to Suzy Sweetman. After we got over the awkward introduction I invited her into the house and we took a seat at the large harvest table in the kitchen. Turns out she was telling my new 'buddy' how excited she was about this tape Randy Hill had given her. It was 'Mom's Kitchen'. He had generously offered to introduce her to me and it wasn't long before we cracked open the beer and started singing, and man could she sing.

My pal Dennis, another writer from Hamilton was over for the weekend and the three of us sat there joking and torturing each other. Dennis was a regular at the house and had been a close friend since the 'Baytides' days. He was a rough looking guy, with a few bad prison tattoo's, but it didn't seem to phase Suzy.

In addition to having a seemingly natural talent for singing harmony, Suzy could drink beer as well. I would play a song then pass the guitar over to her. She pretended to be shy and nervous. Anyone who knows this fine person would say she is anything but. Her short hair and full figure made her seem almost motherly. The afternoon continued in this fashion for hours of laughter, many more songs and a lot more beers. After just a few hours Suzy and I were singing together as if we had been doing it for years. Pammy remembers laying in bed with a bad cold and just having to get up and get a look at this girl who was doing more than just keeping up with Dennis and me. It was the beginning of a cherished friendship.

I too was given to curiosity. The girl seems to be in possession of more than one old soul. She emits kindness and spiritual devotion from one, then swears like a sailor from another. Her singing voice is very soothing to the ear and her personality, fun loving and genuine. If I didn't know better, I would swear that this girl and the Boy have lived more than one life in each other's company. They appear to be overjoyed as if they were two old friends, united after a long absence. I have grown very fond of her and welcome her visits which have become frequent...

Suzy and her husband Pat had just moved to the old Lyco Truck Stop up the road near Princeton. They were both originally from Hamilton and none of us could understand how we hadn't met earlier. We had mutual friends, the same taste in music and the same sense of humor. I recall driving past their place on the #2 Highway earlier that year, before I had met them. They had a home made sign by the road out front that read; 'Clean Phil Wanted'. I told Pam about it and we had a laugh. I was curious to find out if the people living there were just hillbillies or comedians. Turns out they were a little of both. 'Phil' was Pat's younger brother and of questionable hygiene.

The four of us became inseparable. Sue and me would play songs endlessly and Pam and Pat would encourage or mock us for their own amusement. Sue and I would be working on something new and from the other room one of them would yell, "Hey! That song sucks!" followed by uncontrollable laughter.

These armchair critics taught me how to not take myself so seriously.

Sue started getting us 'gigs', not paying gigs mind you. We played funerals, house parties, crashed bluegrass festivals, biker parties, anytime and anywhere. It brought a lot of joy to us and the people around us and for the first time, I understood the gift of music was not all about money or fame. I still craved recognition, but for the time being it was not nearly as important as our new friendship.

People took notice. Word of mouth travels fast. Soon

we were getting hired to do 'opening act' sets in small theaters for bigger acts like Ashley McIsaac and Melanie Doane. The theater setting provided an attentive audience not unlike a small cafe, only with more people.

Together, Sue and I have a brother and sister harmony, and our unrehearsed joking around keeps everyone entertained. We could have them laughing in the aisles or just as easily bring a tear to an eye with a beautiful ballad.

One day, by chance we ran into my old drummer, Ray Ovington. He started sitting in with us on a snare and hi hat. Ray had played with me in KAOS and The Diet. I had been out of touch with him for at least 10 years. Before you know it we were rehearsing in his basement with a bass player.

Eventually Ray's drum kit got bigger and before you know it we needed a sound system and amplifiers to hear ourselves. We added a lead guitar player and "The Honolulu Masters" were born. We were back at Grant Avenue recording a new record. This time with electric guitars, drums and bass. John Lewis had been introduced to me by Mike Northcott. He had played with Ronnie Hawkins and for years with Charlie Major. His guitar sound defines this album. Cindy Dell lived on a farm in Waterford. She had been implanted from Toronto and had a long musical

249

history which included the all girl rock band, 'Tin Angel'. She played bass. Her duo partner, Ron Brammel helped out on acoustic guitar. Suzy and Ray and me rounded it off.

'Full Moon In August' was the first recording of mine to be released on CD. We got some local attention and played some great shows but for now this was just a 'studio band'. I had a business to run. I still had my print/marketing company. Suzy and Ray and I did a lot of enjoyable acoustic gigs on the side.

...He's got five generations,
Of dirt on his hands,
He stares past the cornfield into his dreams,
Bright lights, big city and a five piece band,
Seems so far away,
When you're just seventeen...

FULL MOON IN AUGUST -1996 -FROM THE ALBUM – FULL MOON IN AUGUST

Ray found another bass player, John 'Boomer' Blume and he fit in great. Cindy had her own thing going. Suzy was not comfortable with the 'electric' thing and opted out of this new project. I was sorry to see Suzy go but she had her own passions, bluegrass and gospel, to pursue. It certainly didn't upset our friendship or our regular unscheduled kitchen parties.

I am not privy to the music the Boy plays outside of this house, but I understand it is loud and exhilarating. There is excitement in his dreams and his new songs come to him on the front porch on hot sunny days.

The two old black Labrador's enjoy being the audience and lay content at his feet as not to distract him.

Most of his Sundays are spent here in the company of his fellow songwriters and a tight group of friends. They listen to each others' songs and exchange ideas for improvement. My humble domain has once again become a place of learning...

Ray, John and I got rockier from practice to practice and eventually brought Dan Walsh into the band to play lead guitar. Dan was a local fixture in Port Dover, a tie dyed hippie guitar slinger who played with almost everybody in town. A Guitar Whore, if you will. I really enjoyed this band. It had the same rock edge as my first band but with a rootsy traditional feel and a lot more experience under our belts. I started writing songs for the new band and soon we had enough material for an all original show.

MADELINE

Madeline Bartlett lived two farms up the gravel road behind our home. I can see their old pine bush across the field from my back window. Back in the days when I was hitchhiking phase, whenever I was home, I would visit and help her out around the farm. She had lived most of her life in the little white farm house she was born in. When she got married, the newlyweds moved in with her parents. When her parents passed on they took over the place and when her husband Ralph passed on, Madeline remained. Madeline had been places and done things even though she has lived just up the road all her 80 plus years. She had been to New York City and Boston in the Roaring 20's and from looking through her old photographs, I could tell she was quite good looking. Judging by her collection of old 78 blues records she was also a pretty hip chick. Aside from the little chores, I confess I was there mostly to enjoy her company and listen to her stories. She was living alone and stubbornly independent. She told wonderful tales of another time, like when she and Ralph were dating and they would go to dances in Burford. It was a 45 minute long buggy ride, but most times it took longer.

"Ralph always carried a flask of liquor, which we would finish off on the ride home" she would tell me, followed by a knowing wink.

"Coming home was a matter of getting in the buggy and snuggling under the warm blankets" another wink.

"...and as long as you left the barn door open, the horse would know the way. More often than not we would nod off and wake up in the barn the next morning"

A charming sideways grin would softly light the room as she stared out of the kitchen window towards the old weathered barn as if reliving the moment.
After our small lunch, she would usually ask me for a cigarette.

"But, you don't smoke, Madeline", I would say, and she would always reply, "I know, I know, but I like

253

to have one now and again, they make my head feel lighter, somehow", then she would tell me another story or sometimes I would tell her one...

Jerry Rubin had a book out called 'Steal This Book'. In it there was a section on how to get things for free. One of the sections was on how to get a free 'stone'. According to the article, if you made a tea out of untreated morning glory seeds, the high was similar to LSD and lasted 4 to 6 hours. The south wall of Madeline's house was smothered in morning glory vines, so I related the article to her.

She sat there speechless for a while, and then laughed and remarked, "Well, that explains a lot. I used to bake a morning glory seed cake every season that Ralph just loved, but every time he ate some he would disappear, sometimes for days!"

...I've been gone for, so long now,
Nothin' looks the same,
I went to see her in the nursing home,
She didn't know my name,
But, I sang "So long Marianne",
She remembered every line,
She smiled and held my hand,
Like we never lost the time...

MADELINE
2013 -FROM THE ALBUM -NO FILTER

THE DEAL

Back in the business world I was becoming bored with my job. The print industry was changing rapidly and I didn't see much future for my part in it. It had been fifteen years. Even though we were making a good living, it was time to start looking for an alternative. Something I could sink my teeth into. Something that would challenge me.

On every other trip to Hamilton, I would take time to drop into Grant Avenue Studio, to say hi and catch up on the local gossip in Big Town. Maureen Doidge had become a friend over the years. She ran the office upstairs. I had never really gotten to know her husband, Bob. He kept to himself and was usually busy on a session whenever I came around.

On one of these impromptu visits Maureen confessed that she and Bob were ending their marriage of twenty plus years and suggested that I should buy her half of the studio. I was floored, not only by the news of their failing marriage but by the fact I would even be considered as a candidate for a position such as co-owner of Grant Avenue Studio. The place was legendary! All I could do was give her a stupid grin and reply in my best good fellow voice, "I'll think-about-it".

'Thinking about it' became an obsession over the next few months. What could be better than to have a great band *and* a world class recording studio?

Pamela had grown accustomed to my concerns about the print/marketing business and it's predicted disintegration. Although she knew nothing of the recording industry she recognized the unchallenged drudgery of our current situation. We had fought our way up from the bottom and built a substantial business, but in reality it was the climb that held all of the excitement.

The Boy has an endless amount of numbers in his head. He is trying to assure himself that buying this recording studio is a logical move.

Deep inside the dream I encounter an old farmer reciting a regret I have heard many times, "I wish I had done that when I was your age", he whispers. The Boy remembers his oath to never be one to repeat the phrase.

In spite of applying a cautious business approach to the situation, it is clear he has already made up his mind. Often he has fantasized about having the opportunity to create music in such a place. He will only earn regret if he does not go through with the deal. Pamela senses this as well and offers no resistance...

Taking a blind leap into the unknown seemed more romantic than the middle class mediocrity we had finally achieved. "If that's what you want, go for it", Pamela said.

I dove into studying the ins and outs of running a profitable recording studio in these changing times. It would be a real adventure. The industry was in transition. New digital technology was superseding the old analog techniques and Grant Avenue was in danger of becoming a dinosaur. The recording industry was in collapse and no longer offered much support to new artists. Regardless, I was lured by the exhilaration of getting back into the music business. After looking over the studio's year end statement with a fine tooth comb I decided to kick the can and negotiated a loan to cover the purchase. A certified

cheque was presented on the deadline we had set
and I took possession on April Fools Day 1998. A
premonition perhaps?

The plan was to continue operating my
print/marketing business as well as the financial end
of the recording studio. Then I would ease into the
process of becoming a recording engineer. My
income would come from the the print marketing
company and my draw from the studio would go
directly to paying off the loan. At that rate, the initial
loan would be paid off in two years and then we
could proceed to wind down the printing business. I
already knew a lot about the studio and had studied
digital based recording for years, so I dove in, once
again feet first. The water proved to be very deep.

Bob and I decided that he would take the
responsibility of maintaining the electronics and
mechanical workings of the studio. There are miles
of cable throughout the building that connect the
massive collection of vintage electronics to the
recording desk. Each component needed to be
checked and serviced on a regular basis to insure
everything went smoothly during a session. He
would teach me the ins and outs whenever we had
any downtime. I would take full control of the
business and financial duties.

My initial task provided more challenge than

bargained for. The full financial records revealed the ugly truth. It was discovered that during our negotiations, the lease on the building and the equipment were in arrears. The cost of the lease was choking out any chances of profitability. I had to come up with a solution and drew on the stellar business advice that my old friends and associates had given me in the past. Their practical lessons were not lost on this grateful student. Pulling myself together, I came up with the only viable solution.

My conclusion was that the only option would be to buy out the lease and mortgage the building and equipment. The only hurdle would be whether or not the lessee was willing to sell.

The holder of the lease was a very rich man. His company held court in the Stelco Tower. The highest building in the city. Summoning my courage, a meeting was arranged. No time was wasted on small talk. His time was valuable. I launched straight into my proposal. Mr Zucker sat patiently while I nervously went through the numbers. I had done my homework. My proposal would have me purchase the building and the leased equipment at a fair price and then add the outstanding debt to the bottom line. I gave him my estimates of what the equipment and building were worth on the current market and held my breath. Man, I was shitting my pants. The monthly payments would be considerably less than the existing lease. It was the only logical maneuver at my disposal.

Mr. Zucker was very fair and kind. He was aware that it would be a real problem trying to find anyone who would hold a mortgage on the used equipment. I held my breath.

He looked over my evaluation on both the building and the equipment, sat back, lit a cigar and replied,
"I appreciate your honesty young man, I'll tell you what we'll do. I will hold the mortgage on the equipment purchase, and if you can arrange a mortgage on the building, I will forgive all the outstanding debt."

I froze. Did I hear that right? Should kiss him or shake his hand.

I shook his hand. "Deal!"

The problem was solved. It had taken all of fifteen minutes. I was King of the Fuckin' World! It was all I could do to stifle myself as I made my way to the elevator. The solitary ride down was a combination of fist pumping and "fuck yeahs!" Regaining my composure as the elevator doors opened on the main floor, I coolly walked out into the sunlight. I never had the opportunity to speak to Mr. Zucker again, but will always be eternally grateful.
Welcome to the recording studio business, Mr. Riemens!

GIRLS

The second version of The Honolulu Masters, was Ray Ovington-drums, John "Boomer" Blume – bass, Dan Walsh on lead guitar and me.

During one of our rehearsals in Ray's basement for the 'Girls' album there was a violent electrical storm. We felt safe in our concrete bunker.

Lightning has two defining elements, the lightning bolt coming out of the sky connects with the 'streamers' coming out of the earth. The bolt holds around 60,000 volts of electricity, while the streamer is a mere 6000. In the middle of a song a large bolt struck the television tower on the outside of Ray's house. The streamers came out of the basement floor to meet it and took the shortest path, through our bodies.

"Fuck, Fuck, Fuck!", Dan was using his Fender Stratocaster guitar neck to switch off his amplifier. He thought the shock had come from that.

Meanwhile, I witnessed the incident from my vantage point. Ray let out a grunt and stood straight up from his drum kit. "Fuck!" I watched an electric arc pass from the top of his head into the duct work. In turn he watched the same thing happen to me. "Fuck!" I thought the microphone had been poorly grounded and had given me the shock. It felt like someone punched me in the mouth. I looked to my right and saw our bass player, John crumpled into the corner.

"Holy Shit! John! Are you all right?"

He moaned a few times then weakly answered, "I think so."

The lights in the basement had flickered, or perhaps my brain flickered, but they did not go out and then it was over.

It took a week for our fried nerve endings to stop tingling. We all had third degree burns where the electricity had exited, Ray, Dan and me on our heads, and John on his wrists. I had four broken molars from biting down so hard when I was hit. I was playing a B minor seventh when it happened and still winced for years after, whenever I had to play that chord. For a fraction of a second, the four of us existed on the same celestial circuit.

Seeing as we had survived and I had a recording studio now, it seemed like a good reason make a new record! My fourth. And this time I was at the controls. I had taught myself how to run most of the gear and the board in the first six months with a little help from Bob. The 30 individual channels that make up the console are identical. All you have to do was understand the ins and outs of one track, and the rest are the same. The complicated 'patch bay' that fed the essential outboard gear to the track of choice was the challenge. Determining the ins and outs of the job is a literal reality in this profession.

I believe it is essential for an engineer to learn how to make everything work as seamlessly as possible to keep the flow of the session going smoothly. When the artist gets a creative idea, you don't want to make them wait around while you figure out how to execute it. In order to gain practical hands on experience I looked up my old friend Edgar Breau. He was one of the first writers I met when I first moved to Hamilton. He had been out of the biz for a while raising a young family. In the basement vault at the studio I had found a few rolls of two inch tape, material he had started to work on about 10 years earlier and had reluctantly abandoned. His new family responsibilities had taken over and his disposable income was nonexistent. My suggestion was we finish it. At no cost to him.

We got together once a week for about a year and worked on his project. This gave me a chance to gain the practical hands-on experience I needed without having to worry about being time efficient. Edgar also had to ease his way back into the creative process. The 'win win' approach is a powerful tool to have at your disposal.

The result was the record 'Canadian Primitive' and we're very proud of it. Edgar's raw originality really inspired my engineering skills and I began experimenting with unorthodox recording techniques. I took some on-line courses on equalization and compression, mastering technique and electronics. Slowly beginning to understand the mechanics of shaping and manipulating sound.

After that project, more of my musical friends were enticed to come into the studio during off hours and record for a discount. We ended up creating a lot of gems and I got to hone my craft even more.

Creativity is a marvel that I do not possess. The ability to pull music and rhyme from the air and give it form always astonishes me.

I am a 'chalk on blackboard' teacher.
Repeating to my students numbers and words
that I in turn was taught by my teachers,
without deviation. In my day that was the only
requirement. Morality and business ethics
were the responsibility of the parents. I
confess, I am one of those teachers that has
never left school, although my link to the Boy
has greatly broadened and inspired my
imagination...

The record 'Girls' was a concept album with all the songs about, what else? Girls. A tribute, if you will, to some the ladies that have made an impact in my life. Holley and Lucy make an appearance as well as Bonnie and Alien Jane. I brought in an all star team of session guys to help round out the sound of the core band. We had a great time recording it. This was my first introduction to Brian Griffith's guitar playing and it was hypnotizing. There was so much knowledge to be acquired from these experienced studio musicians and it was only a question away. I soaked it up like a ravenous but grateful sponge.

GRIFF

On the 'Girls' sessions I had asked around who the best guitar player was in town. I was told by many of the session guys that it was Brian Griffith. He had just finished a three year stint with Willie Nelson and played everything from jazz fusion to Motown Soul. John Lewis and Dan Walsh had already put down their parts, but I wanted to add a new texture to a few of the songs. I called him the next day. Brian was more of an artist than a musician. His guitar was his paint brush. Instead of brushing oil on canvas, he tossed color into the air, brilliant shades of red and blue that caress the melody and transform the soundscape. Music is his chosen language, his safe place. Given the chance to express himself he has never failed to dazzle. 'Griff' didn't need to be directed by me, he had much better ideas than I could have ever imagined. He demonstrated an uncanny understanding of the essence of a song. I was intrigued by his unique style and he enjoyed my sense of melody and story telling. This started a close friendship that lasted until his untimely passing many years later.

There is a distinctive taste you get in your mouth when you're high on LSD. It's a little like a mixture of good single malt scotch and tobacco smoke but unmistakably unique. On rare occasions many years after taking the drug, the taste will reappear out of nowhere. It's as if you forgot to lock one of the doors in the endless hallway and a slight breeze has opened it a crack. Flashback time. Sometimes it lasts a few minutes, other time a few hours. When I played music with Brian I was convinced that one of the doors in his mind had been thrown wide open. His face would contort and the magical realm inside would take control of his fingertips. A song we may have played hundreds of times would take on a new, impossibly unpredictable yet wonderful melodic quality. This became my new drug of choice.

...You have to learn how to reach deep and commit when you play music with Brian Griffith. It's as if you're in a speeding car and if you don't dig in, you get sucked out the window...

The sheer joy of living within the moment is not something I am unaccustomed to. I have been escaping to that place all my life, but to witness a group of musical friends and have an audience experience it at the same time is truly intoxicating. To capture it on tape is a rarity. Once again, the 'Girls' album was the best thing I had put out to date, but not being on a label placed it in the underground. One thousand or so copies got out there and that was good enough for me.

I was in love with the recording process and didn't really care for the marketing part of the job. I knew what to do but I felt silly blowing my own horn. I need someone else to do that. I'm still looking. I produced close to an album a year of my own material in my time at Grant Avenue from 1998 to 2010. Each one different from the last. Arguably, the latest one always being the best. 'Blue Martini' was the next album. It was done totally with studio guys and is really well polished. One of the reviews said it was as smooth as a Barry White make out album. It reflects my love of those early Steely Dan recordings and remains one of my favorites.

...So you buy a blue martini, for the lady,
at the end of the bar, by the door,
What were you thinkin' was gonna happen,
why do you even try for?...

BLUE MARTINI
2004- FROM THE ALBUM- BLUE MARTINI

Part of the fun in producing an album for me is also creating the visual artwork. My experience as a commercial artist allows me to do it myself. I take as much pride in the package as I do in the content. Feeling that I was being mentioned too many times on the album credits, writer, singer, producer, engineer etc..., I formed my own art entity, IDEAH, to take credit for the design work. It is an acronym for 'I Do Everything Around Here'.

NASHVILLE

On the strength of a few songs from Blue Martini, I wrangled a small publishing deal with a minor outfit in Nashville. This was thrilling big time shit for me. Fearing that I may never get any major recognition as an artist, I had the hopes that some of my songs could reach a new plateau with a younger, known artist at the helm. Even though I had a huge catalog of material, it was insisted that the best way to get a song 'placed' with a major act was to co-write with an already established writer, a recognized name, someone with a proven track record. I was more than game to give it a try.

Most of my travels to date had been in Canada and this would be one of my first trips into the South. The road was beckoning and a journey into unknown territory re-energized my determination. Arangements were made to cover my ass at the studio for a few weeks and I hit the highway.

...Now it's a two o'clock, truck stop, paper cup coffee,
A tankful of gas and a quart of oil,
A checkout girl with a bee-hive hair do,
Cat's eye glasses and aluminum foil...

65 DOLLARS
2007- FROM THE ALBUM – REDNECK LULLABY

A small furnished apartment waited there for me, right around the corner from the famous 'Blue Bird Cafe' where I had the honor to play a few songs one night. While checking out the downtown area, I spotted a poster. Gordon Lightfoot would be playing at The Performing Arts Centre that evening. Wow! I had just finished mastering Gord's latest album earlier that month. Although, we spoke daily for most of the process, this Nashville concert had never come up. Rick Haynes', the bass player for the band was often a go between when I couldn't contact Mr. Lightfoot, so I gave him a call.

Rick was surprised to hear from me and quickly apologized, "Whatever you need Paul, will have to wait until we get back, we're in Nashville for a concert."

"I know" I said, "I'm standing outside of the

271

theater."

Silence, then a chuckle and an explanation."How many tickets do you want me to leave you at the box office, Buddy?"

"Five would be nice, if that's OK" I replied.

"Done!", says Rick, and after a bit more small talk we said our goodbyes.

Back in my room, I called and invited my new publisher and another writer I was working with to join me as well as the couple that owned 'SOCAN House' where my room was. They were huge fans. SOCAN House provides free lodging for Canadian songwriters visiting Nashville. Everyone met up in front of the theater and I collected my 5 tickets along with 5 all access backstage passes for after the show. A great way to impress your new publisher. When we entered the auditorium I was amazed at the number of recognizable celebrities in the audience.

A Lightfoot show is always performed at low volume, I'm guessing to create a more intimate coffee house atmosphere. When the audience recognized their favorite songs they would sing along in a whisper that reminded me of the sound of wind blown autumn leaves. It was an amazing experience.

Backstage, we mingled with the entourage and one by one the band members expressed shock and confusion when they saw me there. When we finally wove through the crowd to the spot where Gord was chatting and signing autographs, one of my group asked if I would take a picture of him and Gord.

Without announcing my presence we approached Mr. Lightfoot and he posed while I took the shot. When I pulled the camera away from my face, Gord recognized me at once and didn't miss a beat. He gestured towards me and told the small group nearby, "Now this guy can write a song!"

Wow! Now the publisher was doubly impressed! I don't think my ego has ever been so over inflated. What a fantastic way to introduce me to Nashville! Thank you Mr. Lightfoot.

My first trip to 'Music Row' had me feeling more like a wide eyed tourist than a participant. The publisher had set up an appointment to meet another writer in the massive, glass BMI building to work on creating some songs. The first session, although educational proved to be fruitless. My writing partner, Toni Dae, had charted songs for Alan Jackson, George Jones and Tammy Wynette as well as a string of other country stars. My writing style

273

was closer to Steve Earle or John Prine.

The Nashville approach to writing seemed very impersonal to me. Write a line, analyze it, write another line etc... This was 'cookie cutter' shit, but what do I know? I plotted along but it just wasn't me. My style is to introduce all of the elements that make up a song, then go back and edit. A little like sculpting. First, rough out the form and then go back and concentrate on the detail. It works just fine for me.

In my room that evening I wrote 3 new songs that later showed up on my next album. There were many more sessions set up with different writers but the process was the same with almost all of them. It was as if there was some kind of a sacred unwritten rule. I like to make up my own, but that said, I don't believe true art should have any rules. Nothing came out of the writing sessions that stuck, but I insured the whole experience was not a waste of time. I absorbed as much about the craft of songwriting from every writer I worked with.

On my fourth writing trip I sat down with my publisher, Barry.

"This co-writing shit is not working for me man. These people you're setting me up with are all the same. It's driving me nuts!"

Barry rolled his eyes and gave me his best, 'if you only knew kid' look.

"Listen Paul, If you want to make it in this town, you have to play the game. Truth is, if you want to write a hit song, it has to be aimed at 14 year old girls and American housewives with a grade 8 equivalent."

Now, I was rolling *my* eyes.

"We've done the studies!" My eyes couldn't stop rolling... "I'll tell you what. Why don't we try one more thing. I'll set you up in a writing team with four other writers. All the big hits are coming from group writers."

He went on to recite a list of current popular songs just to make his point. I didn't like any of them.

"Let me guess, there will be an uneducated house wife on the team and a guy in camo with a pickup truck and a box of Coors Lite. Right?" I was really starting to lose it, which doesn't happen often but my frustration was taking control.

"That sounds about right." he agreed.

" You know what, Barry? You can take your deal and blow it out your ass! I quit!"

I stormed out of his office and knocked over the life size cardboard cutout of Alan Jackson in the lobby.

"Fuck this!"

Having waited so long to put my hat in the ring really was to my positive advantage. Most of the people I had met in Nashville were much younger, hungrier and more pliable to the demands of the industry, be it right or wrong. The people in charge depend on it, so that they can manipulate you into doing what they think is right. Truth is, they're playing the lottery just like everybody else.

I left Nashville with all the songs for my next album, I had written them by myself. In my room. I felt slightly disappointed and defeated but at the same time elated that I hadn't contributed yet another forgetful, piece of crap song about the flag, or a pickup truck, for the current flavor of the month 'New Country' scene.

Robbie Fulks has a song called 'Fuck This Town' which pretty much wraps it up for me.

BACK TO REALITY

Studio life is grueling work. Long days, long nights. Most of the time enjoyable, but every now and again you get a 'clunker'. After five years it had started to take it's toll. My relationship with Bob, my business partner was strained. Our recording styles clashed. Bob's approach was all about technical perfection, while I put more emphasis on musical performance. We were no longer working as a team. I worked all the off hours I could when he wasn't around. We became separate entities.

To keep my sanity, I imagined Bob and me in a cartoon. You know, the Warner Brothers one with the wolf and the sheepdog.

"Mornin' Bob" I would say as I punched the clock and checked into my locker. I would pull out my sheep outfit and zip it up.

"Mornin' Paul", he would say as he headed for high ground to watch the flock.

Truth is, I wasn't interested in his sheep at all. I was trying to attract more wolves. We are pack animals, after all. This was how I started most of my days.

For the second time in my life I felt hopelessly trapped. It felt like I was riding a dying horse. There wasn't enough money coming in to put aside for an exit plan. We were working from paycheck to paycheck. Whenever there was a small profit to show, it would end up being spent on much needed upgrades or repairs to the equipment. The once thriving record industry was no longer pouring money into developing new product, which left the bulk of our business to small independent productions for fraction of the usual budget. It seemed impossible to just walk away. I had invested our life's savings and taken a blind leap into this business and it felt like I was still in a free fall. I started playing regular gigs to reinforce my meager weekly income and eventually Brian Griffith was playing with me two or three nights a week. My passion for live music gave me comfort. Brian was part of the pack.

Anyone from Hamilton knows about the Mob presence here. Rocco Perry, Pops Papalia, the Musitano's. When you navigate through the Hamilton business and entertainment circles as much as I have, you can't help but run into someone who is 'connected'. One such individual, a restaurant owner had become a trusted friend. He was one of my first customers in the Print/Marketing business and we had become very close over the years. Over a glass of scotch and a beer one evening, I confided in him about my current dilemma.

" What would you do Jimmy?"

He thought about it for a minute and took a sip of his drink, "You got good insurance on this place?"

"Well, yeah", I replied.

" So if there was to be a fire, you would make out O.K. right?" I nodded yes.

" I know some people..."

I stopped him right there. "Jimmy, I love you man, but I think I'll deal with this my way. Thanks for the talk, my friend." and I left.
There are some wolves out there that you just don't run with.

Admittedly, that night in my bed, I fantasized about how the job would be pulled off. But in reality, the next morning, the problem had come no closer to being solved.

THE RAIN

I will now temporarily disrupt the time line and transport the reader, back into the past...

Poooff!..

In our part of the country, way back in the summer of 1990 it did not rain. As much as I enjoy sunny backyard weekend barbecues, the absence of rain was becoming a concern, especially for the farmers in my neighborhood. The crops planted in the spring were burning up in the fields, if they had come up at all. The irrigation ponds and creeks were just muddy holes in the ground. Many of the local water wells were drying up. The once fertile fields behind and around my house looked more like a barren desert.

As a kid, I recall seeing this old Kansas dust bowl movie, The Rainmaker, with Burt Lancaster and Katherine Hepburn. The one where this huckster is bringing his show to the little towns professing he had the ability to make it rain. Of course, he just took their money and moved on to the next mark. I was inspired and wrote this tune on my front porch one afternoon. It was not about magic or small town con-men, nothing like that at all. It was more about the cleansing, beneficial powers of the rain itself. It turned out pretty good.

Weekends on my front porch have always lured company and one hot day in the late August drought, we were blessed to have a few close friends over. Suzy, my old singing partner, her husband Pat and my buddy Rob (we called him Trapper). As was our custom, Suzy and I would sit on the porch swing and trade off songs. Pat and my Pammy were making snacks in the kitchen and 'Trap' was sipping his beer, enjoying the day and the entertainment.

One of my favorite things is to try out new songs in front of this bunch. They pull no punches and if the song sucks, they'll let me know. So I made my announcement and proceeded to play my new 'rain song'. Before I got to the second verse, Suzy had grabbed Pat, Pam pulled Trap out of his chair and they started slow dancing on what was left of the front lawn. The parched grass that remained turning to powder under their shuffling feet.

... There was something much stronger,
Than thunder and lightning,
Just like those old movies, from those two dollar days,
He held out his hand, and asked for a dance,
Immune to the locals, and their go away gaze,
And out the front door, into the downpour,
They danced like old lovers in a holiday dream,
Rosy just smiled, and wiped down the counter,
Those kids aren't as crazy as you think they might be...

RAIN
2000 -FROM THE ALBUM GIRLS

At that very moment, it started to rain. First, big giant drops, hitting the yard, shooting up puffs of dust like tiny slow motion explosions. By the time the song was finished and I joined my friends in the dance, it had turned into a torrent. The tin roof on the porch rattled with the sound of a thousand drums and we were baptized in the glorious deluge.

This dry spell effects us all. Even the old maple curls its leaves towards the sky, beckoning the clouds for a few precious drops to hold in their grasp. The roots of the tree inch further into the earth, searching for a refreshing spring and stretch closer to the surface for their share of the morning dew.

283

*As the dance begins, I am close enough to feel the
soles of their feet...*

There have been many 'movie like' moments on this
old porch but this one lives in my dreams. I was once
again re-born.

Every once in a while, I slide off the tracks. Days like
this give me comfort from whatever troubles I may be
facing in the 'other world'. My dear friends and the
solitude of this old wooden porch have pulled me out
of the abyss many times.

GROUNDHOG DAY

One Saturday morning, the dogs were freaking out again about something by the tree across the gravel road that leads to the driveway.

When I was growing up, a sick skunk or raccoon would sometimes stumble across our yard and Dad would simply pick up a shovel and WHACK!, problem solved. No big deal. He explained that they were sick and most likely had rabies. That said, as I approached the tree where the dogs were making a fuss, I spotted a large groundhog. As the dogs got near, it would fearlessly charge them. "Rabies!" I'm thinkin'!

I called the dogs into the house out of harms way and went back outside determined to deal with the problem. Unlike my nocturnal possum adventure, this time the sun was shining and I was fully clothed. Arming myself with a shovel I approached the terrible allegedly diseased beast, ready to offer up a serving of good old fashioned country justice. He charged me! I dropped the shovel and ran back to the porch, home free and feeling silly.

"That bastard has my shovel!"

Back at the trusty tool shed, I picked out another formative garden tool from the arsenal, a hoe.

"Let's just see who's the boss now" I thought.

I approached him head on, careful not to show any fear, although visions of him chomping on my leg and a series of painful rabies shots hovered in the back of my mind. He charged me again! "Yipes!"

I dropped the useless hoe. In my head I heard a girl screaming, but realizing that the noise was actually coming from my lips, I sprinted back to the safety of the porch.

"OK. Now I'm mad. No more fucking around." I went for my gun.

Unfortunately there were no bullets to be found for the old Cooey 22 and the only other weapon at my disposal was my old Daisy BB gun. I had received it on my 11th birthday. It is a well documented fact that you could put out an eye with it. I convinced myself that one good shot, right in the eye, would put him down.

This kind of unsolicited entertainment is rare in my small domain. I have acquired from the Boy a taste for fantasy and humor. It is a quite enjoyable distraction.

In my fantasy, the ground hog is no other than Merlin himself. The evil Mordred has put a curse on him and he has awakened as a portly rodent. He is old and upset due to his long sleep, angry at himself to have fallen for such despicable treachery. The curious dogs are bothersome but he shows no fear. It confuses his would be attackers.

From across the path he sees the Boy approaching, armed with a shovel. Undaunted, he shows no fear. He charges the knight, cursing and gnashing his teeth, easily disarming him. The knight retreats, only to return with another menacing weapon. Merlin is nothing but annoyed and disarms him swiftly, for a second time...

As I approached, the gnarly beast, it made no effort

to move. Standing on his hind legs he stared me down, looming over my useless shovel and hoe. Undaunted, I crept within 6 feet of him to finish the job. I carefully aimed and fired...

Merlin is growing impatient with this game. The knight, although persistent, does not understand what a formidable foe he has encountered. The new weapon, a musket perhaps, prompts Merlin to summon his magical powers and as the deadly projectile approaches he slows – down -- time and calmly misdirects the tiny musket ball! The knight howls in disbelief and is once again weaponless...

He swatted the BB away like it was a fly and charged me!

"EEIYEEEE!" I dropped the gun and ran for my life. Alone on the porch, I waited there shamefully, in quiet disbelief until the monster finally wandered off. It was my conclusion that the beast had just came out of hibernation and was just simply grumpy. Cautiously, all of my weapons were retrieved and returned to the shed.

Later that day, Pam casually asked, "Did you take care of that ground hog?"

"No" I said calmly, with implied compassion, "I didn't have the heart"

THE WEST TOWN

For 7 years from 1999 on, I played every Tuesday evening at The West Town Bar and Grill on Locke Street as host of a songwriters night. I got to know almost every songwriter in the city. The 'up and coming', the 'been there, done that', and the 'coming back down'. It was The Place to be in this town on a Tuesday Night. You never knew who would show up and you didn't want to miss it.

Brian Griffith would be there on most given nights and sit in with me and the other writers. He lived in the neighborhood, practically around the corner. Members of the Forgotten Rebels and Teenage Head would show up and do their thing. Lori Yates and Ginger St. James would delight the crowd. A lot of the studio musicians would show up to blow

off a little steam after a hot session. The 'Platters'
came by after a show in town and did a few songs 'a
capella' from their table. Occasionally, I would bring
in people that were in town recording at Grant
Avenue. Danny Weis from Lou Reed's Band, Dave
Talbot from Dolly Parton's band, Wardy, the
drummer for Audience. It was a special time. The
format was Original Songs Only, and with
Hamilton's rich musical heritage it was not
uncommon to recognize tunes you had heard on
albums or on the radio.

...The smokers on the sidewalk,
Sway to the rhythm goin' down,
Push back the tables, pour the beer and dim the lights,
Welcome to the West side of town...

WESTSIDE
2009 -FROM THE ALBUM -LOVE IS A DOG

The kitchen at the club was open until 2am and all
the musicians in town knew they could drop in for a
hot meal and a get a chance to hang out with each
other. My new band would do shows on a Friday or
Saturday nights, once or twice a month.

The new band was Carrie Clark, Linda Duomo,
Shauna Dreyson and Randall Hill. Later Brian
Griffith would take over Randall's spot. The
'Barflies' first album was called 'Plain and Simple', a
little acoustic project aimed at getting us into the

festival circuit.

Linda Duomo had been introduced to me when she was 17 during the recording of 'Full Moon In August'. She was Bob Doidge's assistant engineer. Two days into recording I put her in charge. Bob was not on the same page as I was, even way back then, and seeing as Linda followed my instruction without debate I opted to let her finish up. She did a wonderful job. There is a distinctive difference between engineering a project and producing. Unfortunately, most engineers want to be producers. Linda knew the difference. I lost touch with Linda after she left the studio and she was not to reappear until the West Town days, over 10 years later. I grew to admire her songwriting. No doubt, having Willie P. Bennett as a boyfriend and mentor, helped. She became our new drummer.

Shauna Dreyson dropped into my life at a recording session. She had brought in her teenage son's band in to record a few songs. I guided the young band through the process. The youngest member was 14. I did my best to make them comfortable. The 'Hot Mom', sat with me in the control room. Shauna and me connected immediately. I believe that her isolated childhood on the prairies mirrored some of the same dreams and desires as mine. It turns out, she had been a singer back home and it was apparent that she wanted to pick up where she had left off.

291

Four children and three husbands had stalled her progress. I had just recorded 'Blue Martini' and had given her a copy to take home. Almost instantly she started dropping in, twice a week sometimes often bringing food (her East European heritage was showing) and voicing subtle hints.

"I've learned the harmonies for all your songs", she announced on one such visit. "I would love to sing them with you sometime."

"Well, I guess you better join the band then," I joked.

It turns out she was dead serious. There was no backing out. She was in. Now, with Shauna, Carrie and Linda, there were three hot blond babes in the band. How could I go wrong?

I have met these maidens, in the early morning hours in the boy's dreams as he drifts off to sleep. To him, they have become part of the 'pack.' He reviews their previous performance as he slips into dreamland with a smile on his face. He feels a strong bond. Not the same kind as the bond he has with Pamela, but more like the one he has with his sister, Susan. Perhaps musical kinship is a more the proper term, nonetheless, I sense the seeds of permanent friendships have been planted...

'Plain and Simple' and our shows at the West Town got us a gig opening for the legendary group 'Little Feat' at a club in Hamilton. I had been a big fan since the Lowell George days and was thrilled to be on the same bill. At the show, I was helping Carrie bring in her gear from the parking lot when we noticed a young raccoon staggering through the lot towards us. Now, if there's one thing I have experience with, it's nasty critters.

"Don't get near it Carrie" I shouted and gallantly stepped between her and the diseased beast.

"But it looks hurt!" she exclaimed as she went into action.

Suddenly, I'm standing there like an obedient husband, holding her purse as she went after it!

"Carrie! It's probably got rabies! Leave it alone!" but by then she had chased it under a car and was on her knees beckoning for it to come out.

"Carrie! for Christ sake, you're 9 months pregnant and I'm standing here holding your purse!" which I realized, instead of a shovel, hoe or BB-gun was my only weapon. By then we had attracted a small crowd. I reached down and dragged Carrie to her feet and handed her the purse.

293

"Call the Animal Control for crying out loud!" I insisted.

Reluctantly, she finally listened to reason and called them. She was pretty upset when they showed up, lassoed it then immediately gave it a shot of something lethal. I was just happy and relieved that I didn't have to do something heroic. My interaction with critters doesn't always turn out the way I see it in my head.

While all this was happening, Shauna was getting acquainted with Richie Hayward, the fabled drummer for 'Little Feat'. The next thing you know, within a few short weeks, she's moving with her kids to California to be with Richie. Before long they announced they were getting married! Shauna works fast. I admire her. She follows her heart.

The same year, another promoter, Lou Molinaro asked us to open for Howard Werth's band, Audience, which totally floored me. I still believe the album 'House On The Hill' is one of the most innovative rock records of all time. Carrie and Brian joined me for that show. I remember telling Carrie, who had never heard of them, about their influence on Led Zeppelin and one song in particular, "Jackdaw".

At the sound check, Howard Werth, now looking

quite old came on stage, set up a laptop in front of him and strapped on his classical guitar. The rest of the band, a bass player, a soprano sax and the drummer, appeared to be of the same vintage. Carrie did not look impressed. Howard counted in the band and they launched into a full out version of 'Jackdaw'. It was still every bit as heavy as the album version from the 70's, still as unique sounding as it was so many years ago. I looked over at Carrie to see her reaction. Her jaw was literally on her chest. She was speechless.

"Whaaa?" was all she could squeak out.

If you look up a definition of the word 'shocked' in *my* version of the dictionary, there would be a picture of Carrie's face at that exact moment.

REDNECK LULLABY

We had started on the album "Redneck Lullaby" later that year, and I needed Shauna in Hamilton to work on the backup vocals. When I called her in California, I got Richie Hayward on the phone. He was very kind and said he really enjoyed listening to the 'Plain and Simple' album.

"Yeah, Shauna plays it all the time.", he laughed.

"We're starting production on the next album", I said and then jokingly, "I need Shauna to come home and put down her parts and seeing as you stole my singer, the least you could do is show up and play on a track".

To my surprise, he agreed! I think every drummer

in town wanted to be there for that session. It surely was an honor.

> *...I saw a lonely girl, Singing a song,*
> *On the TV late last night,*
> *It's like she stuck a needle in my arm,*
> *And led me to the light...*

IT AIN'T RIGHT
2007 -FROM THE ALBUM -REDNECK LULLABY

During the same time, Linda Duomo was going out with Willie P Bennett, a legendary writer that I had idolized for years. I had done a little work for him in the past, digitally remastering his records for CD, but got to know him much better whenever he came to town to hang out with Linda. He had recently retired from Fred Eaglesmith's band after a heart attack scare. Willie also agreed to come in to sing and add some harmonica on a few tracks. It was Songwriter's Heaven.

We did the album during Christmas break. The studio was closed to the public for the week and most of the musicians in town were on break as well. The atmosphere was like a huge family get together. Lori Yates came by to lay down some vocals. Dan Walsh, who was still touring with Fred Eaglesmith was home to put his parts down. Micheal

297

Fonfara from Lou Reed's Band and Ray Harrison from Cameo Blues Band showed up for a few tracks. It was an open door session and it seemed like just about everybody in town popped in. We even had the pizza guy contribute backup vocals. What a great time we had!

And yet another fine album was released into near obscurity.

You are probably wondering, "If all this shit was so good, why haven't I heard any of it?"

A big part of it is my inability to follow up and properly promote a project when it is completed. I'm usually so worn out by then, I have no desire to do anything about it. I get discouraged when I listen to commercial radio. Will they ever play anything new? Most of the stations spin Classic Rock, or God forbid, New Country God Bless America Crap. According to their scientific surveys, the programmers say this is what we want. Most of the sheep agree.

All I can say is, "Come on!, are those the only flavors you got?"

I keep hoping for a new station to pop up like CFNY in Toronto did in the eighties. They weren't afraid to play something new. It was up to us to decide what we did or didn't like.

I have worked on close to 200 albums at Grant Avenue and at least half of them were stellar. Given a spot in the rotation they could have easily become the 'Classic Rock' of today. Sadly, most of the recordings sit in boxes of unopened CD's, in attics and garages across the country. You may never hear them. The Almighty Keepers of the Airwaves have spoken.

THE FABULOUS BAR FLIES

In addition to our Tuesday nights at the West Town, Brian and I had a weekly Thursday night show at The Cat N' Fiddle, a small room just south of downtown. It was a two year run. Brian and I had integrated our individual styles into one solid entity. The unpredictability of the performances kept it fresh. The audience was split. Half were there for the songwriting, the other to marvel at Brian's guitar work.

There were many sacred brotherhoods that I was aware of before my escape to the New World. The Knights Templar, Freemasons, The Illuminati, all were shrouded in secrecy.

The Boy feels as though he has earned exclusive membership to the 'musically enlightened' when he returns home. One that only a handful of his acquaintances are aware of. His friend and mentor seems to possess the ability to conjure up music from a place that I cannot begin to comprehend. The Boy has been given the gift of understanding that this place exists...

The bartender at The Cat, Lisa, had memorized all of my lyrics. Whenever I got stuck on a line, I could look over and count on her to cue me. When I conjure up a new line for a forgotten one, only she is aware and I am treated with her knowing grin.

It's difficult drawing a consistent audience in a small community like Hamilton when you play so frequently. It doesn't matter who you are, eventually the attendance thins out. On the third season we changed it up and switched to the first thursday of the month. The rest of the thursdays, Brian would fill in with other local songwriters. It was always a kick ass night. Brian's presence guaranteed it, and this format continued.

By now, as a band, we had completed two more albums with Brian on guitar, Carrie Clark-Ashworth on bass and Danny Lockwood on drums. Carrie began showing up for our Thursday shows and most nights Danny or a guest drummer would sit in. We would turn those songs inside out and have a blast watching Brian take them into what seemed like another dimension. Never a dull moment and very seldom, a train wreck. Anyone at the shows could see the sheer joy on our faces when everybody would lock in and nail a new groove. It is as close as I have ever been to heaven.

THE GROOVE

In the studio, Danny Lockwood was my main man. Whenever I required a reliable, talented drummer, I dialed his number first. He reads a song like a scholar reads a book. "Rule number one. Always respect the song" is his motto. He can also read a client in the recording studio and always delivers well beyond expectation. The perfect 'go to guy' for any style of music. He's been a constant on my last 4 or 5 albums and never fails to impress me.

World class talent is hard to come by and the comfort level Danny brings to a show is priceless. He is the true backbone of every band he performs with.

I recall one live show, before sound check, the sound tech told me everything was set up and ready to go including two vocal mics. I was the only singer in the band. The tech informed me that Danny had requested the second vocal mic. Not questioning it, I assumed that Danny wanted to inject some of his humorous banter in between songs. The sound was fantastic, the crowd was groovin' and we were locked in. I thought I was having another acid flashback and was convinced I was hearing the backup vocals that were on the recording. I thought it was in my head, like when you're producing a record and imagine something to add to a mix. I was on cloud nine! Half way through the show I turned around and saw that Danny was actually singing the parts! An additional talent I had no idea he possessed.

THE LOVELY CARRIE

In my twelve years at Grant Avenue Studio, I've engineered hundreds of groups. One evening a bunch of kids walked in to record a demo. Carrie Clark was around 17 years old. She was the bass player. I don't remember much about the band, but was mesmerized by the intense concentration that Carrie exhibited during the session. Two years later she popped into the studio and casually announced she had just graduated from the Mohawk Music Program and if we were looking for a session bass player, she was available. There were already a number of remarkable experienced bass players to choose from at the studio and unfortunately, no room at the inn. Her naive confidence impressed me as much as her trusting smile.

Not wanting to discourage her, I suggested, "I'm putting a band together and you're welcome to check it out" I lied.

I wasn't really putting a band together at all until that exact moment. I just didn't want her to leave empty handed. She enthusiastically agreed.

My style of music is an unpredictable mixture of many elements; Country, Bluegrass, Western Swing, Roots, Rock, and Soul. It has evolved and morphed to a point where I can't put it in a box. Carrie understood the 'Rock' and 'Jazz' thing but had never really been exposed to many of the other styles. Her contribution was fueled by the sheer joy of playing. She kept up with the band on instinct. We would be rehearsing a tune, which I may have thought called for a standard country bass line, and being unaware of the standard, Carrie would play something totally original. Our first practices were a riot. Often I would stop mid tune and ask her to play a line over, only because I had been expecting the obvious.

"Hey! Play that part just before the bridge again, Carrie" She always assumed she had done something wrong. It was *never* wrong. It was different. It was unexpected. It was original and I loved it!

Her confident stage presence, which she was not aware

of, was also an asset. I noticed early on that a large portion of the audience would be watching her and that beautiful youthful aura as much as they were watching me. A powerful, innocent charisma surrounds her like a beacon when she plays.

The Boy feels undeniable love and admiration for this young one. There is a definite connection, a mutual need to intertwine. He cannot conceal it, and this sometimes causes Pamela concern, although from my internal vantage point, I can assure there is no need for worry. The bond is a musical union of two old souls, perhaps siblings in a previous incarnation...

We would play together for the next fifteen years. I can't say I taught her anything by taking her under my wing, but she has become comfortable in her own skin and fearlessly innovative.

Brian's influence affected Carrie with the same intensity as it affected me. She began drawing from the same well as Brian and me. Together, her and I were the rhythm section. We would paint a groove for the lyric and provide a canvas for Brian to bathe in color.

Although I am more than twice her age, sometimes it feels like we grew up together.

307

TOBACCO TROUBADOUR

One evening at 'The Cat', an older couple positioned themselves near the front, listening intently and grinning from ear to ear. At the end of the show I approached them and started a conversation. I was curious. They didn't look like the regular kind of listeners I was accustomed to.

Ron Weiss and his wife Judith were playwrights, live theatre people, and new in town. They inquired if I would be interested in producing a play that involved telling the story of my songs. I was flattered and admitted I didn't know the first thing about what was involved. I gave them my contact number just the same and said goodnight.

As a performer in primarily drinking establishments, I have grown accustomed to meeting all sorts of characters that claim to be one thing or another, a foreign promoter, the brother of a record executive, a movie producer, etc... I don't put a lot of weight on these alcohol fueled conversations. I fully expected to never hear from them again and usually don't. That following Monday though, I got a call at the studio from Mr. Weiss. We arranged a meeting for when I had some downtime, and he and Judith showed up. Ron produced a small portable cassette player and microphone, set it up and started asking questions about where I grew up, what it was like to work in tobacco and how I decided to be a songwriter. After two or three of these sessions he felt he had enough material to get started. I was convinced that I hadn't given them enough pertinent material for a short skit, let alone a play. A month later I was presented with a completed script and the concept.

The stage would be designed to resemble Roosevelt's Dance hall, a popular spot outside of Langton featured in one of my songs. The bandstand would be at the back of the stage, facing the audience. The actors would recreate my growing up stories up stage, presumably from the interior of the dance hall. The Bar Flies'; Brian, Carrie, and Linda and I would provide the music. The four character actors played a much younger me, my Mom, French

309

Godfather, and my girlfriend. The girl playing my Mom also doubled as Holley and the 'girlfriend' was based on the character 'Bonnie' from one of my early albums.

>...Bonnie was a friend of mine,
>With golden hair and eyes that shine,
>At seventeen, a body,
>That sure drove those farm boys wild,
>And she knew, she had something too,
>Pretty soon, she outgrew,
>This small tobacco town, and everybody in it to...

BONNIE
2004 -FROM THE ALBUM -BLUE MARTINI

Ron had applied for and received a grant to get started, and after endless rehearsals the play was launched a few months later for a successful two week run at The Pearl Company in Hamilton.

From my vantage point on the bandstand at the back of the stage, I watched the stories come to life, at the same time observing the audience reaction. It was very emotional and humbling. As a band, it was the coolest gig ever. We got to play together acoustically for fourteen days straight. Two acoustic guitars, upright bass and a snare drum. Carrie and I even had a few somewhat awkward lines.

'Tobacco Troubadour', was well received and more

shows were added in a theater in Delhi, the Tobacco Capitol. The following year we did another run at The Lyric Theater in Hamilton. The entire process brought renewed energy and a fourth dimension to my writing. I am grateful for the experience. The Fabulous Barflies went on to record four albums and to date, they are still four of my personal favorites.

THE EXIT PLAN

By year twelve, I was ready to leave the studio. It was 2010 and It just wasn't fun anymore. The gap had widened even further between me and the daytime crew, Bob Doidge and Bob's assistant, Amy King. Amy had come to us straight from recording school. She was young and pretty. One hundred pounds of East Coast determination. She soon became an excellent engineer, but still preferred to work days with Bob. I was bringing in more than my share of work, but perhaps my exclusion from their daily lives was creating an unhealthy wall of tension between the three of us. I won't dwell on the drama, but let me say this. I was desperate to end it.

I am not accustomed to this turmoil in the

Boys dreams. If there was a way that I could ease his troubles, I would intervene. Perhaps if I were to express a reassurance of well being, presumably as his own inner voice, it may be accepted . If I can keep my identity just slightly below the surface and possibly disguise myself as the muse he speaks of, I may succeed...

Being a part of Grant Avenue Studio had it's perks. Using my 'co-owner card' opened doors and often gave me more slack and respect than I sometimes deserved. It seems everybody wants to talk to you when you're affiliated with a major studio. Of course, a lot of these advantages were lost the moment I handed over my key. Regardless, the true friendships I had earned during my time at the studio remained genuine, the rest of the studio groupies broke ties with me in a heartbeat. A thinning of the flock you might say. But the 'pack' remained intact.

I had many paths that I could follow. I was playing close to 200 shows a year, but that wouldn't pay the bills. In addition to managing businesses for over 20 years, I was a skilled commercial artist, a carpenter, a machinist, a restaurateur. I had been studying guitar building for over 20 years and always had a desire to tackle that as a trade. Of course I could always take a position in another recording studio, but I had grown so weary of the soul sucking grind.

The lone wolf never loses his desire to return to the pack. He has forgotten about the exhilaration of stepping into the unknown. He is somehow unaware of the strong bonds he had acquired over the years. Now speaking as the muse, I remind the Boy of this untapped well of knowledge, friendship and the importance of inner peace...

I had no idea how to get out of this mess or what I was going to do about it, until one cold winter day. I was visiting my old friend, Mikey. His trailer business has grown into a very successful operation and he now employed hundreds of workers. We had been friends since we were 5 years old. While I was 'spinning my wheels', trying to break into the music biz, he was working his ass off at his trailer manufacturing company. He had become quite wealthy.

Mike was showing me his Studebaker truck collection when I commented, "I know you think my job at the studio is really cool, but restoring these relics would be the coolest job on earth!"

His immediate answer was, "When do want to start?"

Mike has always been a man of few words. In retrospect, I had told him about my problems and

314

my desire to get out of a business that I was hopelessly trapped in. He was in a position to correct that problem. That's what friends do. Knowing that our friendship was undeniable, I accepted with gratitude.

It took me a few months to find a suitable candidate to purchase my half of the studio. Selling a business that is barely surviving is not an easy task. I needed to find a person that not only had the money, but was willing to carry the burden of the day to day business. Being honest with every potential buyer, I explained the serious hole in bookings that would occur when I left. This scared off many of them, but finally I found someone with enough money that they were not concerned with success or failure. They just wanted the prestige of owning a famous studio.

The new partner took ownership on April Fool's Day. Exactly 12 years to the day when I had jumped blindly into what turned out to be quicksand. The deal was done! The cheque has been cashed and now here I am in Studebaker Heaven.

STUDEBAKER HEAVEN

Before picking up a wrench and tackling my first project, my task was to modernize and renovate the building that was to become the four bay 'Stude' shop. Construction work comes natural to me. Something in the genes, I guess. The familiar tools; hammer, saw, level and square feel as comfortable in my hand as my old Gibson guitar.

After a month of planning and creating a functional work space, I was ready to begin my new trade. Other than having a soft spot for old vehicles, I had never attempted full scale rebuilds. I had picked up some practical knowledge over the years; mechanics, spray painting, and metal working, but it had been years since I had practiced any of it. With the help of a few online courses on antique auto restoration I was prepared to get my hands dirty.

The Boy takes great joy in building things with his hands. For too long he has neglected his physical talents for the sake of music. He is learning new skills daily and awakening old ones. I share in his enthusiasm as he researches the long lost art of shaping metal with nothing more than a bag of sand and a mallet.

I am transported back to my village, where the local blacksmith is making horseshoes from a single bar of raw steel. The heat and smoke from the forge, the sound of metal hammering metal, the sweat and soot glistening on his face and arms, even on this cold spring morning...

I use my digital camera to carefully document every step, so when it comes time to reassemble there is something for reference. It appears shop manuals for these old relics are almost as rare as the vehicles themselves.

Another valuable source of information is available from the aging collectors and enthusiasts that tend to visit the shop out of curiosity. There is an instant bond, a nostalgic brotherhood and a willingness to pass on many years of acquired knowledge. All I had to do was lure them in by placing an old truck outside in full view from the roadway. It worked almost immediately. These old timers come from an era when all you needed to be a mechanic was a screw driver, five wrenches, a pry bar and some readily available household goods. There has been many an occasion when I have been struggling to remove or repair a part and some weathered old guy walks in and comments, "What you need is a ball of tin foil, a rubber band, and some Vaseline. "That'll fix the prick." They are always right.

I work alone. The solitude is a welcome change from the studio. No sensitive egos to nurse or inflate. No clocks or time constraints. I've got the entire building all to myself, internet, satellite radio and of course, every tool I may ever need. Sweat and muscle, cursing and grunting my way through the day, coming home covered in ancient rust, grease and dust.

My present morning drive to the Studebaker Shop is only 30 minutes, still enough time to prepare before, and to wind down after a hard days work. I still do not carry a cell phone. On my way in, I sometimes take Slant Road to the village of Norwich. On the far side of town they boast their very own Tim Hortons.

This kind of corporate coffee sophistication does not exist in most towns of this size. This is where the retired old men meet every morning to talk weather and politics. They weave tall tales about cats in snow blowers, taxes and their latest medical problems and remedies. I always avoid using the drive through so that I can eavesdrop on their conversations.

The wind down portion on my way home now is only a 'one beer drive'. Sometimes I weave my way down the dirt roads that pass through Mennonite country, north of Tilsonburg. The horse and buggy traffic is anything but hectic. The little kids in their tiny grown up clothes walk home from a one room school with a bell. Sheep are released from their pens at the end of the day to keep the playground neatly trimmed. The ladies, looking like they just walked off a set of "Little House on the Prairie', rake leaves in the front yard in their bonnets and long dresses. A farmer in a straw hat and a light blue shirt with suspenders is walking behind four massive work horses pulling an ancient hay raking machine. Suddenly, this noisy piece of steel and plastic I'm riding in seems very wrong.

Tonight, the Boy dreams of horses, something I am very familiar with.

I am introduced to horseback riding in my 12th

year in the latter part of the 1700's. A neighbor boy has taken it on himself to teach me, unbeknownst to my father, who would not have approved. At risk of losing my virginity, I straddle the docile pony and I am led around the yard by a rope. By the end of the day I have graduated from a trot to a full out run. The speed is dizzying.
My virginity intact, I keep this guilty secret from father for infinity...

All is well in the world. I am working once again with my hands and have the satisfaction of seeing a finished product larger than a CD case. I realized very quickly how this job was similar to creating a great recording. It's all about patience and detail. The time I now spend on music has once again become a source of pleasure instead of something I have to do. It surprises many of my old acquaintances when they ask me, "So, don't you miss being in the studio?" and my answer requires no forethought, "Not for a second!" Other than my own music projects, it never enters my mind. Trust me, taking a two dimensional piece of metal, hammering, folding and stretching it into three dimensional perfection is every bit as artistically satisfying.

The Boy is approaching his 60th year, but his dreams are still that of a young man. I wonder

if this is a common trait in the male species?
His musical aspirations are just as strong, but
the need and sense of urgency has dissipated. I
too have developed an appreciation for turning
a phrase and occasionally, disguised as his
muse, nudge him to write them down. I use
my new found power only with respect and
caution...

The science of swearing is a critical part of the job.
There is no chance of insulting a sensitive ear in my
shop. There are different profanities for every step in
the process. Some require compound phrases.
Loosening a stubborn nut or bolt requires any
guttural word that starts with a 'C', and with blunt
force injury, the more common "Ffuckkk!" or
"Jeezusss!"

I have discovered, in Australia, they have one word
that works in any situation, a minimal approach to
the art form. The word 'cunt' can be applied to
express love, hate, pain frustration or almost any
other emotion, good or bad for that matter. I
remember this when I am at a loss for the
appropriate curse.

I love having the opportunity to expand my
knowledge. Learning something new or having to
repair a piece of lost technology keeps the mind
sharp. 'You've got to work the muscle'. The physical

part of the job has definitely improved my overall health, especially after sitting on my ass for twelve years behind a recording console. Man! I had gotten soft. After about 6 months of pulling wrenches my inner core was restored.

One of the most useful tools for me in the shop is the internet. I have three main rooms to work in; one for disassembly, one for reassembly and one for painting. There isn't a task I need to perform that doesn't have a YouTube video or a forum somewhere describing how best to do it. The second most important tool is the Satellite Radio. Halleluiah! Something I can listen to without getting nauseated. When I'm working on a truck from the 1930's I sometimes access the music of that era for inspiration. It's like having a fucking time machine! New music is readily available in almost every genre. Finally, I get to check out a variety of new artists. It is uplifting. It is inspirational.

My trusty shop guitar is always at the ready for whenever I'm inspired. Often, if I'm misled by a mechanical or electrical problem, I take a break and play a song on my dusty old Ibenez to calm myself down. I start and end every day with a song. It has become a Stude Shop ritual.

This fondness for old vehicles is a disappearing obsession. Most of the collectors are in their 70's or

80's. Their families have no interest in their passion. In this electronic age most people don't know the difference between a carburetor and a microwave, and have no desire to. There are no computers controlling these mechanical wonders, just nuts and bolts and analog ingenuity. The sound of a flat head engine roaring back to life after an 80 year sleep makes me feel God like. I take great pride in what I have achieved so far. I have completely restored four old relics to date. The local car enthusiasts call me The Studebaker Guy.

I seldom see Mikey. He has his hands full running a business with over 400 employees and factories here and in England and Australia. Other than telling me which truck he would like to be next in line for restoration, he lets me do my thing.

THE ONE THAT GOT AWAY

Summertime in Harley provides many home made adventures. On this particular summer afternoon, I was lounging on the porch with my old friend Trapper who was over for the weekend. Trapper is a big guy, over six feet tall. He has cheated death so many times that I suspect he may be immortal. Over the years, motor cycle accidents and work related falls have broken many bones and left many scars. He is soft spoken, extremely well read and his walk, due to his collection of old fractures is something between a Frankenstein shuffle and a John Wayne swagger. An acquaintance of mine from Oakville was coming out to visit for the first time. Maybe it's the lack of appropriate road signs or the overabundance of natural scenery that confuses city folk when they enter my realm, but no one ever seems to get here without some kind of directional challenge. I told Trapper that this time it would be different. I had given carefully planned foolproof instructions to our expected guest. First off, simplify. Coming out of Hamilton on the 403 there are only 3 turns to worry about, left, right and right. Just before my house there will be some kind of road kill to signal your last turn. When you see the carcass, you have arrived. There was always a groundhog, skunk or raccoon festering away just before my corner, but this particular morning the roadway was uncharacteristically free of carnage. "Not a problem", I told Trap, Pamela has just the thing upstairs in her stash.

It has to be understood that Pamela loves yard sales and to date has not been able to pass up on an 'Alf' doll. 'Alf' was that popular alien with an insatiable appetite for cats on the TV series that aired from 1986 to 1990. She gets the dolls for the dogs to play with. In her mind, she mistakenly thinks this will discourage them from chasing the squirrels. The dolls must have been quite a popular item in their day because she has acquired quite a collection of them. I went upstairs and grabbed one out of the box, walked down to the corner and placed it with precision on its back in the gravel just off the road. With the pulse-less landmark in place, the problem was solved, or so I thought.

We were just polishing off the first beer of the day when a farmer came by on a tractor. He spotted the unfortunate animal. Stopping, he dismounted. To our surprise he casually picked up the doll, got back on the tractor and took off!

"What the hell! There goes your road kill!" Trapper chortled.

I was miffed, "There's more where that came from" and I ran upstairs to grab another one.

This new development called for drastic measures. From the garage, I brought out a fishing pole and tied the line to the second wretched doll. Placing it on the same spot about 80 feet away from the porch, I fed the line out so that we could keep watch and maintain control of the bait from our comfortable position by the beer fridge on the front porch.

"That won't happen again" I assured my friend.

A few cars had gone by before one finally stopped. A well dressed lady got out and without hesitation, snatched up the doll and ran back to her car! Trapper had the pole, but didn't react in time. This is a common occurrence with the unfocused fisherman. The woman threw her treasure into the back seat and took off like a shot. "ZZZZZZZZing!" The line unraveled. Trapper had been 'spooled'!

Two Alf dolls!, and now a reel of fishing line was headed down the road to God knows where. We looked at each other is disbelief. Trapper was visibly ashamed. Was the lure of an Alf doll that irresistible to the human species? Apparently so. Undaunted, I ran back into the house and grabbed a third doll. I put some more line on the reel, and proceeded to reset the bait. This time I was in charge of the pole. There could be nothing left to chance. Not only was I going to have to explain to Pamela about the loss of two dolls, but also explain to our guest why my directions were misleading.

"Not on my watch" I sneered.

The very next car was slowing down to have a look. I was ready. I put down my beer, brought in the slack and waited. A big kid, maybe eleven or twelve jumped out of the back seat and ran towards the bait. Just as he was bending down to grab it, I gave it a yank. The doll jerked about a foot onto the road. Startled, he looked towards the porch and our eyes locked, if only for a brief second. Taking me off guard, he lunged and put a death hold on the loathsome soulless beast! The rod arched...

"I got a big one Trapper! Fish on!" I yelled.

J.P. Riemens

The kid was making a move for the car. I only had 8 pound test line so I let him run a bit to tire him out before I started to reel him in. My fishing pole was bent to the breaking point, but I bravely fought my prey. He lost hold for a split second but recovered. I let out enough line to let him get to the car door then pulled back with all my might. He held on for dear life. In the distance I could hear a truck coming. I had him back to the trunk of the car when the transport truck went shooting past in the opposite direction. "Pinggggg" the line snapped. The kid dove into the car and the mother took off and burned rubber. Fate had liberated the plush alien, yet again!

"Shiiit!!" I was going to have some explaining to do when Pamela got home. We sat there silently, in shameful defeat.

The consensus was not to put out a fourth doll. Our enthusiasm was exhausted. My friend from the city ended up getting lost and called us from a town, ten miles away. Pamela got home from yard sailing and among her finds for the day, produced yet another Alf doll. Overall it was a good day.

TRUCKIN'

Thanks to Mike's incurable obsession, he is constantly looking all over the USA for more Studebaker trucks to add to the collection. He takes little interest in whatever I may find. For him, the fun is in finding it himself and closing the deal. I don't bother looking anymore. There are more that 30 trucks hidden in 3 barns already and I had to get a truck drivers license to be able to retrieve his new finds. Now I'm a truck driver, too. My countless road trips have taken me to the four corners of the US and everywhere in between. There is a new catalog of road trip experiences to add to my ever expanding song catalogue.

On one such trip with my old fishing buddy and now trucking companion, Trapper, we found ourselves stranded for 5 days in Lewistown, Montana. I had blown the motor in our truck and we had to wait for another truck to be delivered from Ontario. Lewistown is a small place, as are most towns are in the northwest. There was one music store, where I tried to rent a guitar for the duration of our stay. The young guy at the counter explained they did not rent instruments, "but I'll be glad to lend you one of mine for your stay". Now that's small town hospitality at its finest. We landed a rental car and a few rooms at The Trails End Motel and settled in for the wait.

On our first morning in town, Trap and I went for breakfast at a popular restaurant/casino. Over coffee, I realized that I hadn't locked the doors on the rental car out in the big empty parking lot. Only the hardcore gamblers and the restaurant clientele would be here at 8am. At the car, I was approached by neatly dressed and well groomed young guy, maybe 16.

"Hey mister! Would you like to buy some corn?

I was puzzled. I thought he said PORN! Shady things are quite possible in a casino parking lot.

"Well No!" I said incredulously.

"Well then, how about a chicken and a jar of

pickles?" he replied without hesitation.

"No thanks!" I chuckled nervously. This was getting weird.

I had to wonder what kind of town we had gotten stranded in. Shaking my head, I hastily made my way back into the restaurant.

"Hey Trapper, you won't believe what just happened out in the parking lot!"

As I was relaying the story to my buddy, the waitress caught the end of the conversation.

"Oh, the pickles are wonderful! I bought three jars!" she exclaimed shamelessly.

I was floored but couldn't help but squeeze more details out of her, even though what she does on her own personal time was none of my business. It turns out that the surrounding countryside is home to a Hutterite Colony. They are mostly farmers and often sell their produce in the parking lots in town. The men and boys dress in black jeans and white and black checkered shirts.

Trapper just couldn't get this stupid, 'what an idiot you are' grin off his face'. My shady fantasy had been turned upside down, but it sure was fun while it lasted.

As fate would have it, the main street of Lewistown was blocked off and crawling with people. It was the 25th Anniversary of The Cowboy Poetry Festival. Steak on a pitchfork, quick draw competitions, and enough cowboy poetry to choke a horse. We felt a little out of place. Almost everyone, including the ladies had real six shooters strapped around their waists. The street was filled with cowboy hats and boots. One of the bars was having an open poetry competition, and after plying myself with several 2 dollar American Budweisers, I signed up for a spot. When it was my turn, I simply recited one of my songs to the crowd. There was one that mentioned Montana in it, so I chose that one.

> *...He rode into town on silver and chrome,*
> *Hell in black leather, in a yellow bandanna,*
> *The town, the road, the sky,*
> *Was gray on gray on gray*
> *A black and white photo,*
> *Of a map of Montana...*

RAIN
2000 -FROM THE ALBUM - GIRLS

The crowd cheered! I won free Budwiser's for the duration of the festival.

I am aware of his absence. But the tales of adventure and misadventure provide a great source of entertainment and pleasure. Pamela is equally charmed and on his return, stays up late into the evening with the wide eyed wonder of a young girl listening to a Bard...

LIFE AFTER GRANT AVENUE

I took some of the money from the sale of the studio and put together a good portable recording rig, bought a selection of good microphones and essential software. Other than the actual building, I now have a functional recording studio that fits into the trunk of my car. Which leads us to the next album, 'No Filter'.

A fellow songwriter in Hamilton, Barry Mac, had generously offered his house for the recording. It took a long day to move furniture and wire the setup. We used the couch as a sound baffle for the kick drum and methodically placed carpets and easy chairs to our advantage. I carefully adjusted the frequencies and fine tuned the room. All that was left to do was hit the record button. The band was set up in a wide circle, facing each other. There is more of an incentive to perform to a live audience even when it's just to each other. Strategically placed monitors allowed us to record without using headphones and gave even more of a 'live' feel to the sessions. The stage was set. Brian, Carrie and Danny had never heard the songs before.

In the studio, great players, like everyone in this band, often get their best stuff out on the first take, by the seat of their pants, before they get a chance to over think it. This slightly nervous confidence is evident and adds a realistic live texture to the music. This was to be our honest approach. So, over a beer on the backyard patio, I would play each song to the group on an acoustic guitar so they could chart out the changes. We would chat about what direction was intended and then go inside and knock one off. That album has 7 first takes on it. It is called 'No Filter', truly reflecting the spontaneity of the performance as well as my habitual tendency to blurt out whatever comes to mind without thinking first.

After all that time in a world class studio, here we were in a friend's house with a portable rig, pumping out some great sounding music and having a ball doing it. It took sixteen hours to record and two

335

months to mix and master the album in my living room at 'The Harley Hilton'.

The album won best Alt-Country at the Hamilton Music Awards in 2013. I had been nominated 29 times in previous years for many projects I had worked on, including my own. I have only the one win. Go figure.

BACK TO THE WEST

During my last few years at the studio, my good buddy, Dan Walsh re-entered the picture. He had just finished nine grueling years on the road with Fred Eaglesmith and was doing his best to stay active in the entertainment business. He had built a little recording studio in his house outside of Port Dover and was cranking out some wonderful music. He was also producing records for many of the locals. Finished product would come to me for final mastering.

Fred Eaglesmith has a huge following. They call themselves 'Fred Heads', and Dan's presence in the band for all those years had earned him recognition with a wide reaching audience across Canada and into Texas. We had just finished recording 'Redneck Lullaby' when Dan left Fred's band. I kept bugging him to set up a western tour for the two of us. He had a circuit of 'House Concert' venues set up from Ontario to BC. After some careful planning and a lot more bugging he finally agreed and the two of us crammed our gear and luggage into the trusty Volkswagen Jetta and set out through Northern Ontario, headed west.

This trip was a throwback to my adventures some 30 years previous. I had even managed to add a few dates at the homes of old friends in Alberta and BC. Like me, Dan loves the freedom of the road, leaving your worries behind and looking forward to whatever the next day has to deal out. No drama required.

.
Our show was mix of music and short unrehearsed confrontations between Dan and me, usually ending with one of Dan's, bald headed, tattooed, axe murderer type glares. It kept the audience on the edge of their seats and kind of reminded me of the two old veterans that used to perform outside a bar in Gastown. A little tension, a little humor and a whole lot of music. Thirty days and twenty eight shows later we returned home with our pockets full of money.

Dan is the ideal traveling partner and a constant source of grizzly road stories from his stint on the tour bus with Fred Eaglesmith. He's a trustworthy driver, which comes in handy if you need to sleep. We did a tour a year for about 4 years. My time away from The Bar Flies and the studio was a nice break, although the road can be a grind.

The people you meet at House Concerts are a cross section of music lovers. A lot of them are aging professionals, craving to keep hold of their passion for music. They are reluctant to sit in a bar and wait until 10pm for the band to start while their partner get drinks spilled on them by the drunk 20 year old iPhone slaves on the next table. They are not here looking for a date or a fight. All they desire is a comfortable seat and good evening of song to soothe their musically starved souls.

On one such trip we were in Lively, Ontario, a little town just west of Sudbury. The house was a modern ranch in a newly developed survey that bordered on rock and bush. It was the second stop on our tour. The night before we left, I had watched a documentary, 'The Little Rock Nine'. It was about the desegregation of the school system in Arkansas in 1957. In it, this skinny little 12 year old colored gal faces down an angry mob under the gaze of 1200 armed soldiers. Her courage was inspirational and the production was exceptional. It stuck in my head. Dan and I performed to an audience of 25 to 30 people that night and then went to work after the show, mingling with the congregation. I was commenting on the merits of good Kentucky Bourbon to a group gathered at the dining room table when a tall, gray haired black lady with a southern accent joined in to comment on her favorite brand.

"I'm partial to Old Fitz Prime, myself" she said.

That's how I was introduced to Minnijean Trickey, the little girl from the documentary. I was floored.

Working at the studio, I have met many famous music icons over the years. Being around the business this long makes it less likely to be star struck, but this really threw me off balance. I was suddenly and awkwardly speechless. For those who know me, that doesn't happen very often. The small talk that followed is a blur except for when I remarked on the excellent production of the documentary.

Minni gave me a wide grin, "Then you should meet this lady." she gestured to the person seated beside her and introduced me to the director.

Bam! Speechless two times on the same night! Unheard of!

Two days into the tour and I couldn't shut up about

this meeting to anyone who would listen. It became a segment of our show. Dan would sit back, roll his eyes and check his imaginary watch.

At our first Bar Flies show in Hamilton after the tour Brian, Carrie and I were playing to a full house when a group of older ladies squeezed in. They were having a great time, grooving out in front of the band in the tight space between tables. During the break, I approached them and after introductions it came up that I had just returned from the tour.

One of them asked, "What was the most memorable thing that happened on your trip?"

As I related the Minnijean story the two of them sat there smiling patiently waiting for me to finish.

"You don't recognize us do you?" one of them said.

I shook my head, "should I?".

"Yes you should. We were in the documentary. We were Minnijean's room mates in University"

Triple Bam!

Kay was in town on a promotional book tour and her dear friend Jane had come up from Maryland to help her out. I still see Kay Chornook on occasion. She is

341

a fine author (Walking with Wolf: Reflections on a Life Spent Protecting the Costa Rican Wilderness) and spends half of her time in Costa Rica. I now consider her a cherished friend and whenever she is in Hamilton we try to get together.

THE WAYTOVICH'S & CARRIE'S BIG BREAK

Some of the best audiences you could encounter are in small town Northern Ontario. They are so hungry for good entertainment up there that when anyone decent comes to town they line up in droves. Espanola is one of those gems.

The Waytovich's host one of the rowdiest venues. Pat and his wife Deb are rabid music lovers, as are their friends. You can always count on the brothers, Pat and Donny to be howling away in the front row while the rest of them rock out like they were at a Stones concert. Sadly, brother Donny passed away recently. We will miss him.

One winter, their friend, Doug Vincent hired the Bar Flies to play a special birthday show. This was their first introduction to the full band and to Brian Griffith. They were so blown away with Griff's playing that after the show, Donny gifted Brian a guitar and amp. Brian was overwhelmed with their hospitality.

It was on one of these little road trips that Carrie confessed to us that she was going to leave her husband. He couldn't handle her being out playing all the time. They had been married for about 5 years. I had attended the wedding. They had two small children, one after the other and I sensed he somehow thought that this would keep her in the proverbial kitchen. The musician in Carrie disagreed. That wasn't part of the plan.

Carrie had been pregnant it seemed for two years straight. She was nine months in and overdue when we opened for Little Feat. We actually had another bass player on stand by, just in case. Brian was intoxicated by her maternal glow. On one occasion, he confessed he couldn't look at her and concentrate on playing.

"She looks like a fertility Goddess!" he chuckled.

Carrie had quite often asked me for life advice. She laid out her plan to leave the marriage and I let it soak in. Her idea was to wait for 4 or 5 years until the kids were in school to make the break. All I could think of was the years I had wasted in my broken marriage. I stuck around for similar reasons and later regretted it. I told her the whole story on our trip home.

To my horror, she moved out with the kids the day after we returned. I honestly thought I was just giving her a little wisdom to mull over. Lucky for me and good for her, it was the right move. Carrie's kids have grown up happy and with no apparent ill effects. If it hadn't turned out so good I would still be kicking myself for opening my big mouth.

Tonight the Boy dreams of guilt. He has shared the wisdom of his experience with a loved one and fears he has made a mistake. He admittedly has made some life choices that some people would find questionable, but his affection for the girl makes it almost impossible for him to remain neutral.

Her profound trust in him is not misguided and she reacts without question. I silently applaud her use of this acquired wisdom. Perhaps she will one day, thank him and put his mind at rest...

345

THE WINNIPEG WAY

Espanola, Wawa, Rock Port, Wabigoon, Thunder Bay, Red Lake and Kenora became regular stops for Dan and I in Northern Ontario for the next few years. Ontario certainly hadn't gotten any smaller. Seven shows and a ton of driving in between. Next stop, the 'Welcome to Manitoba' sign to check for messages from our other touring pals, then off to Winnipeg.

Dan had spent a lot of time in Winnipeg working with local Romi Mayes and Gurf Morlix from Texas on an album. He had befriended a large group of fantastic local musicians there, so we always had some form of a reunion party waiting. A club downtown called 'Times Changed' usually hosted. No sign of my old friends Holley and Lucy from thirty years previous.

We stayed at 'Mayor' Matt Allen's house in the North East end. The roughest, toughest part of town. In all my travels, this was the first place that I ever felt like I was in danger. That feeling wears off after a few visits and you get used to the sounds of shouting and breaking glass. The police tape and burned out buildings just add to the charm. It's sad to see the number of native people who have come here to improve their lives or sometimes to disappear and end up strung out on whatever substance, so far away from being in a better place.

> *...Police tape and razor wire,*
> *Gangs that set your house on fire,*
> *and streets, you don't want to walk alone...*

WAITING FOR THE BOOM
2010 -FROM THE ALBUM – DIRTY SUNSET

There are a growing number of good people moving into the neighborhood though. A collection of artists, musicians and regular folk, just trying to get a leg up, proud to own their own homes and doing their best to improve their surroundings. There is honor in this disarray. If you live here, your neighbors, who or whatever they are, look out for you.

We were playing downtown at a bar called The

Stanton. I went out for a smoke break after the first set and got into a conversation with a tall, attractive red head. I commented on how the music scene here was just as tight as the music community in Hamilton.

She just laughed and said, "I know exactly what you mean. I'm originally from Hamilton. I was here for five years before I realized I had left"

I still love this town.

FLAT LAND

As expected Saskatchewan offered an uneventful drive, although we played in Weyburn to the south. On the way there you pass through the town where they filmed 'Corner Gas'. The Ruby Cafe stands deserted. The old grain elevator still announces the fictional town of Dog River. On our way through the province, the spring thaw had flooded out the Trans Canada Highway and we had to detour for hours around it looking for dry land. The entire place as far as you could see, and that's a long way out here, was an expanse of red, muddy water with the odd road poking through.

My favorite trip through the flat lands was on what would be my last tour with Dan Walsh. We were heading back east from Alberta and stayed over in

Medicine Hat. The couple there hosted 'The JarBar Concert Series'. There was no show scheduled but they were kind enough to feed us and put us up for the evening. It was great to discover, even after 30 plus years that Alberta hospitality has not diminished.

Our next stop would be Winnipeg, so there was a long day's drive ahead of us, straight through Saskatchewan. After we said our farewells and boarded the trusty Jetta, Dan produced a bag of magic mushrooms he had saved specially for this occasion. It was a fine ride, drifting through the flat province, high as kites with J.J. Cale blasting through the speakers. I saw a lot more beauty than desolation that day. Every stop was an adventure, thanks to Dan. Even stopping for a sandwich at the Subway store proved to be entertaining. I remember floating down the barren road thinking to myself, Jesus, look at me, 57 years old, stoned on mushrooms and touring the country. I couldn't wipe the grin off my face. I kept a watch out for the flipped over spinning car with the laughing people from my first trip years ago. I wonder now, if this type of travel could be a regular pastime in the prairies. If not, I'm sure it would catch on.

I am familiar with the story of the spinning car. I regret not being in range to experience this magic substance they have ingested. I long

to find myself in the well furnished room.
Given the chance, I would open the door for a
face to face conversation or perhaps, a dance. I
would appear this time as the Muse, of
course...

Changing directions to the west and back to the first
tour, we entered the British Columbia interior.

My little brother lives in Vernon, BC. It is his home.
He has put down roots. Ron had arranged a show at
a friend's farm outside of town. In addition to the 40
people there, I got a chance to hang out with my
niece and nephew, which was fun. Brother Ron is no
stranger to a party and all of us got pretty wasted
after the show, except Jessie, my niece. Jessie is tiny,
almost pixie like and reminds me of a young Avril
Levine. She had agreed to be our designated driver
in Ron's old '72 Chev Camper Special. We rode in
the box with the equipment, and Jessie, who was
barely big enough to reach the pedals and look over
the steering wheel would shout out whenever we
had to duck down so the cops wouldn't stop us.
The next morning we began our return trip, back to
Red Deer Alberta.

Burford Gas jockey and Bob Marley fan, Andy
Jeans has lived in Alberta longer now than in our old
home town. Andy has also re-rooted himself. He had
arranged a show for us at his place. This was their

first house concert and Andy and I had talked at length on the phone over the previous months on how best to pull it off.

Andy is on his third marriage, and with his present wife Laura, has finally found someone who can tolerate his sense of humor, not unlike Pam and me. At 50, with two grown children, Andy and Laura have started a new family and have added another two wonderful kids into the mix. The two of us still have regular 'phone parties' two or three times a year. We tie up the lines for hours. A bottle of Scotch on my end and a bottle of Jameson's on his. When he first moved to Alberta we would send each other elaborate hand written letters complete with crudely drawn illustrations. They were hilarious. I wish now I would have kept them, but back then we had no idea his move would be so permanent.

His house has become a desired stopping point for most of my touring musician friends and many I don't know. He and Laura put on the best shows on the circuit, sometimes once a month. Laura loves to cook and most of the shows are like 'dinner theater' performances. The local radio station CKUA even talks about the 'Jeans Off, House Concert Series.'

CKUA is publicly funded radio station and plays throughout the province of Alberta. It is truly the best radio station in the country. The only one I can listen to. CBC sucks. This station plays new music and has shows hosted and programmed by real music lovers. They do live interviews with independent musicians like me, who are trying to make a living in a tough market. I'm certain if there were a radio network like this in every province, new original music would have a fighting chance. If you are ever on the prairies make sure to tune in. You won't be disappointed.

I still haven't found anyone to replace Dan on these little excursions. Dan has become a respected songwriter and along with his great playing has an entertaining solo act, even though he has no one to argue with. He keeps himself booked solid around Ontario and still takes the trek out west at least once a year.

It's been a long three years since my last tour. One of these days...

SINGING TO THE COWS

When I was a kid, I would take my guitar over to
the bridge and play for the dairy cattle that hung
out by the creek.
All dairy farms have radios in the milk house and
the cows get accustomed to music at milking time.
Some farmers could just crank the radio and the
cows would file in through the open door.
I knew this fact, but still, I played for them
and they would stop munching on the grass and
wander over,
to stare up at me with those big admiring eyes...

Our shows at The Cat in Hamilton had become a full blown band gig. Drums, bass and two electric guitars. I had switched to my old '53, 125 Gibson with a small amp so that I could hear myself over the drums. It turned out to be a good move. We sounded like a real band. Four people, combined to create one sound.

In the current bar scene there are not many true bands. Most full time players have to sit in with 4 or 5 other acts just to pay the bills. The era of the tight, well rehearsed groups has been replaced with loosely structured jam bands. My group was beginning to suffer from the same affliction. Every member of the Barflies played with other bands. Even me, I toured with Dan and did solo shows. However, in our case we had the passage of time to keep things sounding coherent and a regular gig at The Cat. We had been playing together for 15 years. My only complaint was that it had become increasingly difficult to book new gigs and work around everyone's busy schedule.

I've always had backup employment, so I could afford to devote all of my free time to my own projects and I was feeling frustrated with my inability to introduce new material to the group. There were at least twenty new songs in my guitar case and regardless of our familiarity with each other, I was reluctant to rehearse the new songs in front of a live audience. Asking for rehearsal time was asking them to cancel other paying gigs. There was a defined direction I wanted to take with the new recording and it was unlike our previous albums. Some things you can't just sort out on the fly.

When the same core group of musicians are spreading themselves so thinly, every act in town starts to sound like the same group with a different singer, which in fact it pretty well is. I wanted something that would stand out, not blend in. Perhaps this desire has been a detriment to my career, but I have never been a follower of trends. What I do is what I do. It is a result of respecting the past and putting in the work to honor the future. Trends weave through time, rise and fall in popularity. True art is timeless.

DARK CLOUDS ON THE HORIZON

The band had just finished one of our monthly Thursday night concerts in Hamilton. As usual, it was a kick ass show. Brian, Carrie and I exchanged our traditional hugs. We had torn down our gear, split the money and said our love yous and goodbyes.

Two days later while preparing a meal with Pammy, I got a call. It was from the my pal Lori Yates, the Queen of Cowpunk. I gave her my usual cheerful greeting. When it wasn't returned with the same enthusiasm, I knew something was wrong.

"Brian Griffith died last night. I didn't want you to

find out on the internet" she stuttered.

I still recall the dead air on the phone while I tried to process what I had just heard.

"Thank you Lori" was all I could muster and I hung up the phone.

I sat at the kitchen table, speechless. My body had turned to stone. Pamela's intuition told her something terrible had happened. She did not ask what, only embraced me from behind. After a time I shuddered and told her the news. I truly thought that after losing my child thirty years ago that nothing could ever hurt me again. I was wrong. Now, writing this passage three years later, I find an ache in the back of my throat and a tear in my eye as I try to write this down. Brian was and always will be a defining part of who I have become.

Resilience is something I always took pride in, but perhaps age wears the edges off. "Jump back in the boat, or drown", I told myself. I forced myself to go about my daily routine but I felt like an empty cup. Three months later I finally booked some shows. My time at the studio had introduced me to the best of the best and I enlisted a number them to fill in for my fallen brother. None of them came close. I realize now, it was unfair of me to try to compare anyone to Brian. It was unfair and impossible. I just couldn't do it any more. I folded the band.

I had a dream last night.
Brian and me had pooled up our cash and got a
cabbie to drive us as far as the money would take us.
We ended up somewhere
on the lonely number 8 highway.
I had no idea where we were going or why.
I became aware that this dream was just as real as
anything that could happen in my waking hours,
and it filled me with joy to be in his company.
We had our guitars, but didn't play,
just talked and laughed,
for what seemed like hours as we walked down the
deserted road...

-perhaps he still exists behind one of the doors in the
endless hallway.
I woke up with a smile on my face.

*I witness this dream. I am there. At first
puzzled. I feel I am violating a sacred
brotherhood trust. Their conversation and
laughter is as fluid as the music they created
together and I realize another spirit has been
granted access to the Boy's dreams. The reason
for the visit is not at first apparent, but it has
gifted him a profound peace. If being not so
afraid of revealing my presence, I would have
joined them in the walk and welcomed the*

visitor, but I remain unnoticed...

Our local haunt, The Cat had asked if I would do a Songwriter's Night. They needed someone to fill in their Monday evenings and I agreed. "Back on the horse, Bucko". I stuck it out for the next 12 months. The turnout was respectable and there were a few inspiring moments but the spark was missing. I still wonder if the reason for the sporadic attendance was because it was held on Monday night or was it because I hadn't fully recovered from the loss of my dear friend. People instinctively seem to avoid the grieving.

...There is a level of comfort and trust that comes with playing with the same people for so many years and in my advancing years, I fear I may never experience that feeling again.

I was 59 years old and suddenly had no interest in booking any more shows. I needed to step back and sort out what to do next. In the past, I would just hit the road to re-invent myself, but I have created strong ties that I know can never be broken. A little voice in my head told me this setback would be resolved in due time.

STUMBLING
THROUGH THE VOID

Music is a powerful engine and creativity fuels the beast. Over a year had passed without performing but the coals were still glowing, just waiting for me to provide the needed oxygen. You just can't turn this shit off. It was time to put my new songs to the test.

I had my recording rig ready to go. My friend Jon Kloepfer, Mike and Sandy's son, had built me a powerful computer designed to my specs to capture the production. The songs were meticulously arranged and charted. All I needed was the right band.

I turned to my old drummer Danny Lockwood to help. He has always been there when I needed him.

Danny has an instrumental jazz trio with a few other guys. Paul Intson is the most creative bass player I have ever worked with. He is to the bass what Brian was to the guitar. We share a common interest as Paul is also a mastering engineer. Before I got into it myself, he mastered my first CD, 'Full Moon In August'. Eric Boucher is the 'insane Frenchman', originally from Timmons, Ontario. He attacks a keyboard as if his fingertips are hardwired to his brain. He has played on many of my recordings dating back to the early 90's. I enlisted my friend 'Deeps' to overdub the organ parts later. All these fine players are drawing from the same well that Brian had given me directions to many years before.

I wondered what my Americana/Canadiana Singer Songwriter style would sound like with this killer group as the backup band. Different than the rest of the crowd, I'll bet. My Motown roots reminded me that the backbone of most of those old hits were also created by jazz musicians, The Funk Brothers. The goal was to create a unique piece of work without suggesting the limitations of an individual style. After selling a few of my precious guitars, I had enough cash to fund the project. The plan was to track the songs at Paul Intson's home studio in Ancaster, closer to the rest of the group than my place. The mixing and overdubs would happen at The Harley Hilton.

You could define me as a passive producer. When you are blessed with the best artists around, you're better off exploring their input before making suggestions. A little nudge here and there is all that is required. Drums, bass, keyboards and my rhythm guitar. The lack of lead guitar was not by accident. Completely unaware of it, I was still struggling with regards to my early attempts to replace Brian.

Transtar Deluxe was the result of this unlikely combo. The title comes from a Studebaker truck. It was such a change from my previous efforts, I had a real challenge mixing it. I wanted this album to really groove. A collection of songs you could drive to. All my mixes were road tested in the car, driving the back roads to the Studebaker Shop. I really struggled. Hours turned into days and months. It could be because mixing music was no longer an everyday thing for me in the years since I left the studio. It could be that I loved all the sounds so much that I was reluctant to assign them to their proper place. It could be that the absence of Brian had me looking for something that was no longer there.

This process often goes unappreciated, but to me, it's the difference between a good record and a great record. It doesn't help that I am my own harshest critic. Regardless, the finished product was released almost a year after tracking it. I'm very proud of it. Great grooves, great band. I believe all my work has a common thread, even when the configuration of the band changes drastically. In the end, it's all about the song.

It appears a great deal of energy has been expended on this project. The Boy has not dreamed in ages and when he does, it is incoherent. I have tried to reach him during his waking hours but to no avail. The emotional release he expected this project to achieve has not come to pass. The effort has left him exhausted. Although he tries to maintain the positive, I fear his grief still has a firm hold. He has misplaced his desire to create. There is no spark...

THE ISLAND

Even though I may not see my oldest friend for months at a time, Mikey seems to instinctively know when things are not right with me regardless of the brave face I choose to present. It's almost as if he has an inner receiver that picks up my frequency. Only true friends possess this power.

The new album had been released but once again I lacked the ambition to follow up with the necessary steps to promote it. I was physically and mentally drained.

"What is the point?" I wondered.

The number of people buying CD's has dwindled down to a few hard core music fans. Most people under the age of 40 don't even own a CD player or a decent stereo. I think, deep down I was just relieved that I got it finished.

"One step at a time" I told myself.

Living in this negative funk was affecting my work in the Studebaker shop and at home. I started smoking cigarettes after 15 years and turned more and more to alcohol to grant me dreamless sleep. When I did dream, they were just reruns. On occasion, I could sense a whisper of reason or encouragement but it was too far away and too weak to comprehend, like trying to pick up a conversation from across a crowded room.

> *...I smoke too much, I drink too much.*
> *I eat too many chicken wings,*
> *I've been a fool for the loving touch,*
> *Of one too many pretty little things,*
> *One day it's gonna kill me,*
> *Gonna lay me in my grave,*
> *And all I've got to leave behind,*
> *Is the money that I didn't save...*

YOU CAN SAY N0
2016 -FROM THE ALBUM -TRANSTAR DELUXE

Mike and Sandy had just purchased a 5 acre island in the Thousand Island chain of the St. Lawrence

River. It boasts an impressive 11 bedroom summer house complete with two castle like turrets and a huge covered porch. The house was built by the Canada Corn Starch founder, Mr. George Benson, in 1901. It is a masterpiece of woodworking and stone work. I was asked if I would be up to living on the island for the summer, to keep an eye on the work crew and restore the porch.

"A change is as good as a rest." my Dad used to say.

I jumped at the challenge.

While the carpenters, roofers and masons did their thing, I busied myself with the task of completely reconstructing the ancient porch. The porch is 120 feet long by twenty feet deep and incorporated into it are the two huge round rooms at the bottom of the turrets. One round room encompasses the living room and the other opens out into the endless porch.

It is a stimulating task to recreate with authenticity. You have to first remove the skin and inspect the bones. It's hard to imagine something this perfect was constructed without the use of power tools and modern laser assisted measuring devices.

Old Peter, my dad had taught me many of the forgotten building methods when I was still a kid. I had to dig deep to open the doors in my memory, the rusted hinges were reluctant to comply after over 40 years of immobility. Once inside, the answers were surprisingly simple.

Dad had always said, " All you need to be a builder; is a hammer, hand saw, a level, a square, and a chalk line. Square and level is the key."

The old timbers speak to me in an almost forgotten language, like an old song on the outer edges of my memory. Most of the structure and the interior woodwork was created on site by former shipbuilders that had traveled up river from the ship yards in Montreal. Their craftsmanship was no longer required at the turn of the century with the introduction of metal hulls. The flawlessly sculpted paneled walls and ceilings are reminiscent of the interior of a luxurious tall ship. The original leaded glass curves around the circular rooms, distorting and transforming the river view into a Monet painting.

At 4pm everyday, the rest of the work crew hop in their boats and go home to the mainland. I am left to myself, encompassed in this ancient piece of history, surrounded by the imperial pines that tower above the structure overlooking the mighty St. Lawrence. The solitude is heavenly and complete. The hammering and swearing throughout the day, therapeutic.

Come evening, there I was, alone on a deserted island with my guitar and a collection of new songs. I began reconstructing and arranging them for solo guitar, trying not to lose the feel of the recording. Tough work when you're used to having a band sort that stuff out. All I ever had to do was strum along and sing. After so many years I suddenly had to pay attention to my guitar playing. Concentrating on the musical hook lines and bass runs, I painstakingly attempt to commit them to muscle memory. I certainly didn't want to be one of those solo performers playing the same maddening rhythm to every song in their repertoire.

The eight servant staff of the former owners had lived on the third floor. Their spirits still wander the halls at night and on occasion I catch sight of a face in the dimly lit hall mirror. They seem to have grown content with my playing and rarely bother me. I had originally set up my portable studio up there in the top of one of the turrets, a round room with a unfinished timber ceiling that reaches up in the middle like an Indian tepee. Their presence was so overwhelming up there that I had to move my stuff back downstairs where my privacy was more respected. I developed a habit of announcing out loud, my retirement each evening and wish them all a pleasant "good night."

369

My bed is in the former kitchen staff room at the back of the house, next to the pantry. On more than one occasion I have been awakened by a sharp knock on the door at 6am. Two raps, 'knock, knock', even though I am the only soul on the island.

I always replied, "Thank you! I'm up!"

It seems the Boy has become sensitive enough to feel the presence of entities other than myself. Possibly his time in solitary or his advancing age has made him come to realize he is not alone after all.

I know nothing of ghosts or spirits. I merely exist within the confines of the old maple and on the pages of this story. He has come to appreciate that when he fills the air with music an audience is always present, living or not. A wonderful incentive to grow and improve. His dreams have returned and it appears that my passive encouragement has in some small way been acknowledged...

REDISCOVERING THE NEED

After filtering through all of my recordings, I came up with a list of 70 songs to work on and painstakingly re-arranged them for the solo show. I was surprised by the vast amount of material that I have created over time. Some of the songs re-awakening emotions that had been long forgotten. After a few months I had narrowed it down to the 30 to 35 tunes I would need for a live show.

Having a large collection of guitars, I have them placed so that whenever the muse beckoned, I am ready. There are two hanging in my living room at the Harley Hilton, one in my Studebaker shop, one in the Island house and another at Mike's place in

Arizona. I'll never be a lead guitar player but my rhythm playing is by no means boring and is constantly getting better. I am ready to perform. I put the feelers out to all of my old haunts.

I was alarmed to discover the current practice for a lot of the clubs was to book ahead for the year. I hadn't counted on that. Now I had to wait for the beginning of the next season to get back into the loop. Although content with my current status, it's always an incentive to work harder when you have a show on the calendar.

I speak to the Boy more frequently now. It is the same young boy I met so many years ago, even though his body is witnessing the effects of age.

He has grown comfortable with disappointment, realizing the yin and yang commands an equal amount of success. He is also acceptable of the little voice in his head and welcomes the company.

There was a time I had wondered if indeed I was making contact or perhaps the Boy's actions have just been coincidence. After all, I still have a desire for purpose. It troubles me that other spirits are not aware of my presence. If so, then what am I other than just words on a page?

I seem to have developed a closeness that is obvious even in his day to day activities . Working alone, he often speaks to someone other than himself, and ponders if this may be a symptom of age that will magnify until he is the old man in the park apparently talking to no one as the children point and giggle...

Being the social animal I am, there has always been a level of discomfort performing music by myself. Rehearsing alone for the last few years has now become the norm. I play my songs in an empty room, somehow aware that I always have an audience, even if not in physical form.

There is something gratifying about delivering a piece of music in its purest state. If the song doesn't deliver with guitar and vocal, it just isn't a good song. I had spent 12 years in the recording studio with other artists and have come to the conclusion that if you don't have a good song to start with, no amount of production can save it. You can add backup singers, a horn section, some killer keys and a screaming guitar, but without good lyric and melody there is no point. You can't shine a turd. This is one of the reasons I don't have any desire to go back to recording other people in the studio. There are an endless supply of bad songs out there and

J.P. Riemens

people with money that want to record them. I'll leave that uninspiring task to my old studio associates.

THE AWAKENING

On the eve of my 60th birthday my life suddenly began to make sense to me. I have spent almost 50 of my years pursuing a dream and in some small way have achieved my goal. The music created flows through my veins and has become as familiar to me as putting one foot before the other. I have been on this quest for so long that it has become as natural for me to write, play and sing, as it is for my heart to beat and my lungs to draw oxygen. I still dream the same dream as when I started this journey and it still gets me out of bed every morning. My younger friends see me as a bit of an oddity, a young man's soul in an old man's body, and I wonder if I will ever grow up. I tend to forget I have passed my expiry date until I catch my reflection in a mirror or a shop window.

Most of my audience has grown old as well. The music industry has all but collapsed, but the people that created and supported it in it's prime still require the groove.

I was playing a house concert in Red Rock, Ontario to a group of white hairs and instinctively toned down my delivery and filtered out some of the songs that I thought might be offensive. After the show, one of the guests was complimenting me on my songwriting and I told him what I had done. He chuckled and reminded me,

"Son", he said, "We are children of the 60's and there is nothing you could do or say that would shock us."

In that moment I became aware that I was not alone.

As the boy dreams, I observe that in this state he is almost always a young man and I envision myself as the same young woman that landed on this continent so long ago. In a spiritual sense, I desire the comfort and warmth of his company. I am now certain that he is aware of my presence and he no longer troubles himself trying to make sense of it. He accepts this feeling with gratitude and grins like a child witnessing a magic trick when he hears my whisper. A child of the 60's, indeed...

376

I no longer address the physical age of the people I encounter. I speak to their spirit. My 85 year old mother, Rita, giggles like a school girl when I speak to her in this manner. My sisters tend to talk to her like she is a helpless child but I know now, that deep down, she too is still the same young woman that loved to flirt and dance.

Being focused on a dream can sometimes cloud over the success of your reality. A great home, a tight group of old friends, a companion that has been with you for more than half of your lifetime. I possess all of these things and yet somehow I feel I have not met my full potential. My adventure is far from over. It may just be beginning.

This realization has awakened a new chapter in my existence. I still dream, but now my goals are much broader. Music will always be the center of my efforts, but I have other passions that spark my imagination. I am possibly the only person on the planet that gets paid to exclusively restore Studebaker trucks. This spills over into my love of restoring historical architecture and more recently, my interest in writing stories and books. It all fits together, like an elaborate mosaic. The doors have flung open and once again, I start every day with enthusiasm. The soundtrack that accompanies my purpose has been transformed from a three minute song into a symphony.

THE VISIT

My brother Ron and his kids have made their way to Ontario this Christmas season. Jessie and Chris are in their mid twenties now and are true British Colombian natives. We had a series of sleepless, laugh filled nights and consumed mass quantities of adult beverages. It was the highlight of the year for me. The day they left, Ron handed me a special present he had brought all the way from his home in Vernon. A large helping of magic mushrooms. At the time I remember thinking to myself, who do I have to share this with? I couldn't think of anyone. Pam has never had a desire to take any kind of mind altering substance and just rolls her eyes when I suggest she try it. I put my treasure away in my 'cookie tin' where I keep my pot and papers when I have any, and put it out of my mind.

About a month into the New Year, I decided it was time to try it out. It was a Friday afternoon and I had come home from a full rewarding week at the Studebaker shop. Pam was working into the evening and wouldn't be home until 8pm. As a personal service worker, she cares for the sick and elderly in their homes and often works late hours. I would always make sure to prepare a nice meal for her at the end of the day.

My grand idea was to do the mushroom now, and by the time Pam got home around 4 hours later, I would be in a reasonably controlled state. I cracked a beer and ate half of the mushroom while I started preparing the meal. By the time I had finished my first beer the main course was in the oven and the timer set. I made a small salad and peeled some carrots, put the carrots in a pot with some water and salt, and set it on the stove, ready to turn on when it got closer to suppertime.

At around 7pm I started to feel the full effects of the mushroom. I welcomed the pleasant glow and sat back to soak in the experience. After a short while it was time to start the carrots. I went to the stove, turned on the burner and went to the bathroom while I waited for the water to boil. This is when I got a good look at myself in the mirror and realized just how high I was. This was awesome!

Every molecule in by body was vibrating and I declared, out loud, "This is the best Friday, ever!"

The Boy has taken some magic substance and I find myself in the same elaborate room as I had appeared in twice before. This time, I am a woman of 40 or 50, maybe 60. My long hair is peppered with gray and tied back with a colored ribbon. I am wearing blue jeans and a billowy white shirt, tucked in at my slim waist. I spot the door from across the room and proceed to it with confidence. Without thinking, I open the door and step through...

...I am in the boys living room. He has just finished constructing a paneled ceiling and I stand there in the center, aware of the rug beneath my feet, looking up, admiring his work...

On my way back to the kitchen, I caught a glimpse of movement in the living room. I assumed it was my old Lab, Bronson but when I look in to see, there stands a woman! Her age is hard to determine, but she is barefoot and dressed in jeans and a white shirt, and she was staring at the ceiling, smiling. I reminded myself of my present condition and remained calm.

"What do you think?" I said.

"It's beautiful"

She continued looking at the ceiling.

"Do I know you?"

"Oh, Yes"

As much as I have longed for this conversation, I do not want to disrupt the spell and choose to be brief.

Deep down I recognized her knowing smile as one would recognize an old friend. Her eyes were a familiar deep green I was certain I had seen before. I had a feeling that she belonged here as much as I did.

"I'm sorry, I don't remember your name" I inquired,

"My parents named me Elizabeth"

"Well Elizabeth, what can I do for you?"

Her eyes widened, as if surprised by hearing me say her name out loud.

I felt as if I was in a trance and struggled to find the words.

381

J.P. Riemens

"Would you play me a song?"

When she spoke, it held hints of a forgotten accent that I could not identify and for some curious reason reminded me of a warm spring breeze through the trees. She looked at me as if she has known me in the light as well as in my darkest moments.

"What would you like to hear?" I asked.

"Please play 'Untouchable', I like that one"

At this point, I'm thinking that maybe I had eaten too much of the mushroom, but what the hell, I was really enjoying this. It didn't even occur to me as odd that she would know one of my songs. I picked up my guitar and sat on the couch and began play...

> *Don't you try to break my heart,*
> *I can do that by myself,*
> *You don't have to try so hard,*
> *I already know who you are...*

Free from my anonymous chains, I feel like a young girl again and as I take in a breath of the sweet fragrant air, I outstretch my arms and dance with unrestrained joy.

> *...Take a breath from your lover's lips,*
> *You can't hold it in your hands,*

So I just stutter, stumble and trip,
On your invisible terrain...

As I played, she danced with the grace of a ballerina, twirling and making delicate gestures with her hands. Trails of soft blue smoke follow her every move.

...What you are, Is a dream I've had all of my life,
What you are, is the difference between wrong and right...

The sun setting in the west window cast no shadow and illuminated her porcelain skin like a candle through milk glass...

...What your are, is untouchable...

The song was over. I was breathless and just sat there staring in awe. She glided over to the couch and sat beside me. When she touched my hand, I found myself instantly transported to the top of the old maple tree out back. I was not in the tree, but inside of it. The view was breathtaking. I heard her soft voice surrounding me as if it emanated from inside...

"Your carrots are burning"

"Th- thank y—wha? Oh Christ! The carrots!" I had

totally forgotten!

I jumped up. The kitchen was full of smoke. I turned off the stove and opened a door to clear the place out. I tossed the pot into the sink and filled it with water. When I went back to the living room, she was gone. The spell was broken. A single red maple leaf remained on the floor where she had danced. I gently picked it up and placed it safely between the pages of my songbook.

At the risk of being admitted, I did not mention any of this to Pam when she got home. I had managed to salvage supper and carry on a normal conversation. After she retired, I treated myself to a big glass of Scotch and a bad Sci-Fi movie. I went to bed with the last remnants of the mushroom coloring my thoughts. As I drifted off, the last thing I remember was staring down an endless hallway with an infinite number of adjoining rooms. One of the doors stood open...

ADDENDUM

That was to be my final chapter for now, but yesterday I received a letter from my home insurance company. It seems they are concerned with the proximity of the big maple tree behind the house. The tree I call Old Mother. According to educated estimates, it is somewhere in the neighborhood of 350 years old. It looms up and over the house and they feel that catastrophic damage would be imminent if one of the large branches should detach itself. They inform me that if I do not have it removed, they will be forced to cancel my insurance.

I have cultivated a great disrespect for the insurance industry, it's legalized extortion, if you ask me. I tell them to go fuck themselves.

"If the tree goes, I go with it."

A day later, apparently reluctant to lose my current monthly payment, they withdraw the request.
The Lying Bastards.

In my head, I hear Old Mother thank me in a voice that is not mine. It sounds surprisingly familiar.

"Thank you Boy" it whispers.

"You're welcome, old friend" I say aloud, to no one in particular.

THE END

ABOUT THE AUTHOR

J.P. Riemens still resides in the old school house in Harley Ontario. The ancient maple tree still towers over the graveyard out back, where Elizabeth Watts gravestone sits.

He has recorded 12 full length original albums with appearances by Willie P Bennett, Richie Hayward (from Little Feat), Michael Fonfara (from Lou Reed Band) and many other notable Canadian artists.

You can find out more at www.jpriemens.com